MAKING
CHEESE

CHEESE.

1—Gorgonzola. 2—Double Gloucester. 3—Koboko. 4—Parmesan. 5—Dutch. 6—Roquefort.
7—Schabzieger. 8—Dunragit. 9—York Cream. 10—Port du Salut. 11—Cheddar.
12—Pommel. 13—Camembert. 14—Mainzer. 15—Cheshire. 16—Stilton. 17—Cream
Bondon. 18—Gruyère. 19—Wiltshire Loaf. 20—Cheddar Loaf.

MAKING CHEESE

MAKE YOUR OWN TRADITIONAL ARTISAN CHEESE, BUTTER AND YOGHURT

SUSAN OGILVY

BATSFORD

First published in 1976 by Batsford

This edition first published in the United Kingdom in 2015 by
Batsford, an imprint of Pavilion Books Company Limited
1 Gower Street
London WC1E 6HD
www.pavilionbooks.com

ISBN 9781849942720

A CIP catalogue record for this book is available from the British Library

20 19 18 17 16 15
10 9 8 7 6 5 4 3 2 1

Reproduction by Mission Productions Ltd, Hong Kong
Printed and bound by 1010 Printing International Ltd, China

This book can be ordered direct from the publisher at the website:
www.pavilionbooks.com, or try your local bookshop.

Distributed in the United States and Canada by Sterling Publishing Co., Inc.
1166 Avenue of the Americas, 17th Floor, New York, NY 10036

Some of the cheeses described in this book:

1 Smallholder cheese (see page 90)

2 Lactic cheese (see page 68)

3 Mysost cheese (see page 85)

4 Crowdie (see page 70)

5 A cream cheese (see page 83)

6 A Cambridge slice (see page 80)

7 Colwick cheese (see page 79)

8 Coulommiers cheese (see page 71)

CONTENTS

MAKING CHEESE

There is increasing interest today in home-produced food: people everywhere are growing their own vegetables, brewing their own beer and wine, baking their own bread. This book describes how it is also possible to make cheese at home, without any very complicated equipment or special premises. Susan Ogilvy explains in detail the techniques for making hard, semi-hard and soft cheeses. She gives step-by-step instructions for many delicious delicacies: fresh milk cheese, cream cheese, traditional soft cheeses such as Crowdie, Colwick and Cambridge, the larger Smallholder cheese and the Small Cheshire. She also describes how you can make other dairy products at home, from yoghurt and butter to fresh clotted cream.

Although the book will obviously interest those considering farmhouse cheesemaking who have a ready supply of milk, and people who are aiming at self-sufficiency, it has been written specifically with home cheesemakers in mind, food lovers and others who obtain their milk from the local supermarket.

Home-produced cheese has a unique flavour that no shop product can imitate. By making cheese at home, you will not only save money but will enjoy a fascinating and very satisfying craft, with a delicious and nutritious end-product.

Note for American readers:
The American equivalent for the British single cream is light cream. Double cream is heavy cream and sultanas are raisins.

AN INTRODUCTION TO
CHEESEMAKING

THE HISTORICAL BACKGROUND

Cheesemaking is an ancient craft – one that goes right back to the beginnings of civilization. The first cheeses were probably made by early nomadic tribes on the borders of Europe and Asia. These tribesmen knew that if a food was dried it was easier to carry and was also preserved for longer in an edible condition. Milk could be partially dried by being left in a shallow vessel to evaporate in the sun. The warmth caused the milk to sour and an acid-curd cheese was formed. Perhaps rennet-curd cheese was later discovered by happenstance when milk was carried by tribesmen in bags made from animals' stomachs.

Cheese was a favourite food of the Ancient Greeks and Romans, and various ways of making it developed. Its nutritional value was recognized too, for in Sparta wrestlers training for the Games had to include it in their diet, and the Roman legions used to carry cheese as an essential food ration on their marches. The Romans also influenced the development of cheesemaking in Britain; during their occupation cheese became a popular food. A description of cheesemaking written at the time shows that they had a good understanding of hygiene, the use of rennet, and the draining, salting and storing of cheese. The general methods used then changed little over the years until the nineteenth century.

The early cheeses were of a soft type; gradually ways of making harder cheese, which kept longer, were developed. Methods were handed down from generation to generation, mainly by word of mouth. The ways to obtain the best results were learned only by trial and error, and important factors such as the development of acidity were little understood. It was not until the nineteenth century that scientific principles were applied to cheesemaking: the different varieties were classified and methods were standardized for making them. The variety of cheese came to be identified by the name of the region in which it was made or marketed. Today comparatively few of the varieties remain; some are extinct and others have merged. On pages 22–25 there are details of the main sorts of cheese available in this country today.

THE PRINCIPLES OF CHEESEMAKING

Milk is a unique food. At times, because so many different products can be made from it, it seems almost to be endowed with magic properties. Before beginning to make cheese from milk it is important to understand a few of the principles involved, and how the properties of milk make cheesemaking possible.

Two properties of milk are important in cheesemaking: (i) liquid milk can clot to form a semi-solid curd, and (ii) milk can sour and become more acid.

Milk owes its ability to clot to the presence of a protein called casein; casein is relatively hydrophobic and precipitates – separates into a solid – when rennet is added, or when the milk turns very acid. When this happens the milk becomes blancmange-like in consistency, forming a curd in which liquid whey is held, a process known as coagulation or clotting.

Rennet is a substance found in the stomach of young mammals, which enables the milk – their first food – to form a clot so that it can be easily digested. This is why the milk clotted when the early tribesmen carried it in bags made from animals' stomachs. Since then man has extracted the rennet and used it to make cheeses and junket (a traditional milk pudding made with milk and set with rennet – sometimes honey, sugar or lemon was added).

Rennet works best when the milk is warm and contains soluble calcium. Milk naturally contains calcium in a soluble form, but if it is boiled or heated to a high temperature this calcium becomes insoluble, and the rennet will not work. This explains why you cannot use boiled, sterilized or ultra-heat-treated (UHT or 'long-life') milk to make junket or cheese.

Rennet also works best when the milk has soured and is slightly acid. Milk owes its ability to sour to the presence of lactose or milk sugar. Lactose can be changed to lactic acid by certain bacteria, and this increases the acidity of the milk. Lactic acid-producing bacteria use the lactose for growth and ferment it to lactic acid. They are naturally present in raw untreated milk and cause normal souring when this milk is kept in warm conditions for some time. However, they are not present in sufficient quantity in pasteurized milk.

Most milk now sold in the UK undergoes pasteurization, a heat treatment which destroys all the disease-causing organisms and ensures that the milk is absolutely safe to drink. Pasteurization also kills most of the lactic acid-producing bacteria present in the milk, so improving its keeping quality. Therefore, with pasteurized milk, a special culture of lactic-acid bacteria has to be used to start the souring process. The use of a culture also helps to ensure that the growth of bacteria is carefully controlled. The cultures used in cheesemaking are known as cheese 'starters'.

Rennet curd forms the basis of most hard and soft cheeses. But, as mentioned previously, the milk protein can be precipitated solely by high acidity (the acidity needed is much greater than that required in order for rennet to work). In such cases a bacterial culture is again used for the production of acidity, and the resulting acid curd is the basis of acid-curd cheese, yoghurt and other cultured milk products.

When the milk has been coagulated either by the rennet or by high acidity, the resulting curd is treated in various ways –

depending on the type of cheese being made – in order to release the whey. Whey consists mostly of water and lactose; the fat and other constituents of milk remain caught in the curd with the protein.

Acidity continues to develop throughout cheesemaking and is a vital part of the process, particularly (as will be seen) in the making of hard cheese. It helps to give the finished cheese its flavour, and also checks the growth of other organisms which could be harmful, thereby acting as a preservative.

An Introduction to Cheesemaking

THE MANUFACTURE OF HARD CHEESES

There are many thousands of varieties of cheese made throughout the world, but these varieties can be grouped into different types according to their method of manufacture and ripening, and their physical properties. In the UK most national cheeses are of the hard-pressed type, such as Cheshire, Cheddar or Lancashire, so we will discuss first the basic steps involved in the making of a typical hard cheese.

These hard British cheeses became known as territorials and a grading system evolved to measure quality and consistency. During the Second World War and immediately after, much of traditional cheesemaking was lost, to be replaced by bland block cheese made in factories on an industrial scale. By the early 1970s, farmhouse cheese production had been reduced to less than 50 or 60 farms in which it was made or marketed. Today, thankfully, the picture is very different – there are numerous examples of excellent traditional British territorial cheeses as well as hundreds of modern artisan cheeses, thanks to a revival in farmhouse cheese making which began in the mid-1980s, due partly to the introduction of milk quotas in 1984.

Certain fundamental steps are the same for almost all hard cheeses, and only small changes in these individual processes produce the different varieties. The flavour and texture of the finished cheese are determined by slight differences in times and temperatures, in the weight of pressing and the length of maturing.

Souring or ripening the milk Starter culture is added to warm milk in large cheese vats. The milk is left for about 45 minutes to sour or ripen. The development of acidity at a steady rate is very important in the making of hard cheese and must be carefully controlled throughout the process in order to produce a good cheese. The development of acidity at various stages can be judged by physical changes in the curd, and these are learned only by experience. However, now the commercial cheesemaker can also measure the acidity by means of a titratable acidity test, which measures the percentage of acidity. Kits are available to the small producer, are relatively inexpensive, and are essential if you are planning to make cheese for sale and also if you want a degree of consistency in your product. PH meters are also available to measure acidity but require calibration regularly and accurate meters can be really quite expensive. The use of a reliable starter culture helps to ensure the development of acidity at a steady rate.

Renneting Next the milk is heated to about 29–35°C (85–95°F); and rennet is gently stirred in. If the cheese is to be red, colouring is added before renneting. The milk is then left for about one hour or so to coagulate.

Cutting the curd When the curd is firm – like a firm, milk jelly – it is ready for cutting. Horizontal and vertical bladed knives are passed through the curd to cut it into pea-sized cubes and free much of the whey that is held in the curd. After the initial cut once both ways, the curd is left for a period known as 'healing' for 5–10 minutes, before commencing further cutting. This allows some whey to precipitate and the curds to firm a little. This rest period prevents what is known as 'curd dust', which will be lost in the whey when it is drained off and will subsequently reduce the yield of cheese.

Scalding the curd The curd pieces floating in the whey are heated slowly to about 38°C (100°F) over a period of about an hour. Increase the temperature by approximately 1°C every 10 minutes to avoid case hardening. (Case hardening occurs when a skin forms round each particle of curd and prevents the whey from precipitating out of the curd, leading to wet cheeses with off flavours developing in store.) The curds are stirred continuously.

This 'scalding' process causes the curd pieces to shrink and helps to release still more whey. The continued development of acidity in the curd has a similar effect, and the rate of this development is important. If the curd develops acidity too fast, instead of forming firm and resilient pieces it becomes an unmanageable mass and pulls out in slimy wet strings. If the acidity is too low the curd will remain soft and sweet and will retain moisture, so that the cheese will spoil later by releasing moisture after a few weeks. The cheesemaker must keep a proper balance between the acidity and the moisture content of the curd by adjusting the degree and length of scalding and whey drainage. If the curd is developing acidity too fast it must be drained of whey more quickly by scalding it to a higher temperature over a shorter time; if the curd is 'working slowly' slow scalding to a lower temperature will result in slower whey drainage.

Draining the whey After scalding, the curds are stirred for the appropriate time and then stirring ceases, allowing the curd to settle (this is called 'pitching'), and the whey is then run off. As the curd settles it consolidates and shrinks. It is cut into blocks which are piled, turned and re-piled on each side of the cheese vat, leaving a drainage channel for the whey. During this draining period the curd consolidates and shrinks further, and the acidity increases. The curd changes in texture.

Milling and salting the curd The curd is milled – broken up into small pieces – and salt is added and well mixed in. Salt is added at a rate of 1.8–2.5 per cent depending on the type of cheese and is well mixed in. It helps to preserve the finished cheese and to bring out its flavour. The salt also expels further moisture, stops any more lactic bacterial activity and is involved in the secondary maturation process.

Moulding and pressing the curd The curd is next packed into moulds and pressed for varying lengths of time and under varying pressures depending on the variety of cheese. Once out of the press the cheese may be greased with lard or vegetable fat, or bandaged. These bandages can be removed and the cheese allowed to dry naturally for a few days before dipping in cheese wax several times to give three or so coats of wax to ensure that it keeps properly.

Maturing the cheese Finally the finished cheese is placed in a special room to ripen and slowly mature. This room is kept at a temperature of 10°C (50°F), with a relative humidity of 80–90 per cent. The steady temperature ensures even ripening, and the correct humidity prevents shrinkage of the cheese due to evaporation. The cheese is turned every day at first and then less frequently later. During ripening various chemical changes occur which provide the flavour and texture of mature cheese. These result from the action of bacteria and enzymes in the curd. The bacteria in the 'starter' culture contribute to the process. Enzymes present in the rennet continue slowly to break down the protein, making it more digestible and the cheese mellow. The cheese becomes firm and the rind more definite.

Types of hard cheese

There are a wealth of new and traditional English hard cheeses widely available now, distinctive in taste, colour and texture.

Cheddar, Cheshire, Derby, Double Gloucester and Leicester are hard pressed, so they have a relatively low moisture content and can be left to mature for a longer time to achieve their full flavour. There is nothing to beat an English Cheddar if it has been well matured. It needs at least three months; a good Cheddar is usually ripe at six months and mellow at nine months.

Lancashire, Caerphilly and Wensleydale are semi-hard cheeses. As they are only lightly pressed they are moister and quicker to ripen than the hard-pressed varieties. Continental hard and semi-hard cheeses include Edam and Gouda, Gruyere, Emmental and Parmesan.

The characteristic blue veining in Blue Stilton (and other 'blue' cheeses) is caused by a harmless mould which grows in the air spaces and cracks in the curd. The curd is not pressed but packed loosely into hoops. Aeration may be increased by piercing the curd with wires. Again Stilton is best eaten when fully ripe, not less than six months and preferably nine months after it has been made.

SOFT CHEESES

A number of different types of cheese can be classified as soft cheeses; they are characterized by their small size and their comparatively high moisture content. The curd is drained slowly without pressure, by gravity, and therefore has a high moisture content compared to the pressed varieties and is quicker to ripen.

True soft cheese

This is made from fresh milk which is coagulated by rennet. The development of acidity is not as crucial as it is in the making of hard cheese, and a softer curd is formed. However, starter is usually added just before the rennet and gives a clean, acid flavour to the resulting cheese. The rennet takes longer to set the milk because there is no acid development at this stage; the acidity develops later during the slow whey draining process. The curd is ladled into traditional moulds or hung up in muslin bags and allowed to drain slowly for up to several days.

At one time there were many English soft cheeses but only a few have survived. These are usually eaten in a fresh or unripened state at a few days old. In European countries soft cheeses are very popular and there are a wealth of different varieties. Many of these – the well-known Camembert and Brie cheeses are examples – are ripened. As we have seen, the slow ripening of a hard-pressed cheese is due to the action of bacteria in the low-moisture curd; in soft cheeses, surface moulds are the major agents and grow very quickly on the moist, acid surface. The moulds secrete certain enzymes which break down or digest the curd and produce the characteristic texture and strong flavour. The ripening proceeds towards the centre until there is a soft creamy mass throughout. You can tell the ripeness of a soft cheese by pressing the middle and feeling the softness at the centre.

Ripening soft cheeses require critical temperature control at each stage, a warm atmosphere initially and then cooler – 4–8°C (39–46.5°F) – as it ripens. Humidity is vital: 85–95 per cent RH (relative humidity) will encourage the mould growth. The desired moulds may be present in the atmosphere of the particular cheese factory, or the curd may be sprayed or inoculated with an appropriate culture.

Acid-curd cheese

Acid-curd cheese is another type of soft cheese although not a true one, since rennet is not used to coagulate the milk. Acid-curd cheese is formed solely by the action of lactic acid upon the casein. This acid curdling is completely different from rennet coagulation, and gives a curd of high acidity, quick drainage properties and granular texture. The curd is usually drained in a muslin bag. The cheese will not ripen on storage and should be eaten when very fresh. Lactic cheese is an example of an acid-curd cheese.

A note of warning is needed here. In the past acid-curd cheese was traditionally made from milk which had gone sour. However, this was raw milk which had soured 'normally'. It is not advisable to use pasteurized milk which has soured or gone off for cheesemaking or in cooking. Pasteurized milk keeps for longer because nearly all the lactic acid bacteria are destroyed by the heat treatment. If it does go 'off', this may be caused by the growth of other bacteria which could be harmful. It is always wiser to throw such milk away.

Cottage cheese

This is made from skimmed milk from which the cream has been separated. Traditional British cottage cheese, such as Crowdie, is not the same as the American cottage cheese you can buy in a carton. The American version is made from skimmed milk coagulated by acid; the curd is washed several times to produce the characteristic separate particles.

Cream cheeses

Cream cheeses are not really true cheeses since they are made from gravity-drained cream. They have a rather granular, spreadable texture, a rich, creamy, mildly acid flavour, and can be moulded into various shapes and sizes.

THE NUTRITIONAL VALUE OF CHEESE

Cheese has an excellent nutritional value; it is one of the best and most economical protein foods, and a very good source of calcium. It is therefore an important food for children, especially if they don't drink much milk. But cheese can play an essential part in the diet of the whole family, both young and old. It is extremely versatile and can be eaten at any meal of the day, including breakfast, or as a snack, cooked or raw. It goes well with both sweet and savoury foods, as the protein in the main course, or as part of the dessert.

So make sure there is plenty of cheese in the house – and good cheesemaking!

A NOTE ON DAIRY HYGIENE

Before starting to make cheese it is a good idea to be aware of the dangers which may arise unless proper care is taken. Because milk is such a good food it is also an ideal medium for the growth of bacteria and other micro-organisms. Special attention must therefore be paid to ensure that the milk and utensils used are thoroughly clean, and to prevent any chance of contamination. Not only will the taste and appearance of the products be spoiled, but the growth of harmful bacteria could well cause food poisoning.

To help avoid these dangers you should read particularly carefully the sections on the heat treatment of milk and its subsequent cooling (page 44), the sterilization and care of the utensils and premises used (pages 37–39), and the cultivation of a reliable cheese starter (page 49).

Most especially, if in doubt as to the quality in terms of food safety of your produce, throw it away!

HUDSON'S
DRY
SOAP

HUDSON'S
DRY
SOAP

EQUIPMENT

EQUIPMENT NEEDED FOR MAKING SOFT CHEESE

The equipment needed for making soft cheese is relatively simple, and much of it can be improvised from ordinary kitchen utensils. It is worth spending a bit more on those articles that you do buy to make sure that they are of good quality. A list of suppliers is given on pages 138–140 and there are many other excellent suppliers on the internet. You will need the following:

Thermometer A proper dairy thermometer. It must be graduated from 0–104°C (32–220°F). Inexpensive digital or dial probe thermometers are widely available from dairy, kitchen or catering equipment suppliers.

Room thermometer This is useful for checking the temperature of the area in which you make cheese, incubate starter or store the maturing cheese. Maintenance of the correct temperature is important. This thermometer can be obtained quite cheaply from a chemist or hardware store.

Measuring jug A 2-litre (4-pint) measuring jug is useful to measure out the necessary quantities of milk or cream.

Mixing bowls An assortment of 1-litre (2-pint), 2-litre (4-pint) and 4-litre (6-pint) capacity bowls are required to hold the milk. The size needed depends on the type of cheese being made and the quantity of milk involved. Ordinary Pyrex mixing bowls are suitable, but stainless-steel bowls can also be obtained.

Buckets For larger quantities of milk use a 10-litre (2-gallon) capacity bucket. Stainless steel is best – never use galvanized iron or zinc, or aluminium, as these corrode. A strong plastic dairy bucket will withstand most of the temperatures used; is easy to sterilize and cheaper than stainless steel.

Water bath The milk should nearly always be heated indirectly, in a water bath. The water bath can be an ordinary saucepan provided it is larger than the bowl containing the milk. Larger bowls or buckets can be stood in a sink of hot water – you can top up the water in the sink with more hot water from the tap.

Cheese cloths These are squares of cloth used for draining the curd. You can make them yourself from good-quality butter muslin bought from any fabric shop or online. They should be about 45–60cm (18–24in) square and of double thickness. You will also need some odd pieces of string to tie and hang up the muslin draining bags.

Some equipment for cheesemaking.

Spoons, syringes, ladles and knives A long-handled spoon is needed for stirring the milk; a tablespoon and a teaspoon for measuring cheese starter and rennet; a perforated spoon and a soup-type ladle for ladling curd; a knife with a long blade for cutting the curd. Ordinary kitchen utensils are quite sufficient, but they should be of stainless steel. A set of plastic measuring spoons – ¼, ½, 1 teaspoon, and 1 tablespoon – will be useful for measuring small quantities, while syringes give accurate 10ml and 20ml measures for rennet.

A plastic or stainless-steel colander This makes the task of placing the curd in the cheese cloth much easier. The colander can be lined with cheese cloth, placed over a bowl and then the curd can be spooned into it.

Moulds These can be of various types. Traditionally the different soft cheeses were each made in their own type of mould (see the section on making soft cheeses on pages 60–85). You can improvise with empty plastic food-grade containers with holes drilled in the sides and bottom. However, smallholding suppliers and cheesemaking supplies stock a wide variety of plastic moulds available in small or large quantities. They will last you many years, so a small initial investment is definitely worthwhile.

Square cake tin with the base removed.

Cocoa tin with the base removed and holes pierced in the side.

Improvised moulds.

Straw mats and cheese boards

Cheese boards These are used for placing the moulds on while the cheese is draining. Plastic chopping boards or trays that are easily washable are ideal. The actual size will depend on the size and number of moulds you are using. For example boards 33 x 18cm (13 x 7in) will hold two Coulommiers moulds or two 15cm (6in) square moulds for Cambridge cheese; boards 18cm (7in) square will hold one Coulommiers mould or one Cambridge mould at a time. Online shops or discount stores are useful when improvising. You will need two boards of each size.

Draining mats These are used on the boards for drainage purposes. They should be of the same length and width as the boards – improvise with straw table mats cut down to the right size. If you cannot obtain suitable mats, folded cheese cloths can be used.

Draining matting can be bought on the roll sold by the metre, which you can cut to size for your needs. The mats are place on top of the boards. They can be easily washed and sterilized between batches and are considered more hygienic than the traditionally used wooden boards and straw mats.

Container for collecting the whey When making soft cheese in moulds there is a continuous flow of whey, and a container in which the cheese board can be placed is needed to collect the liquid. A washing-up bowl can be used to take longer cheese boards.

Scales These are useful for weighing the finished curd. Ordinary kitchen scales can be used.

Small screw-cap glass bottles for starter recultivation See the section on cheese starter, pages 49–58.

A cheese press.

EQUIPMENT NEEDED FOR SEMI-HARD CHEESE

You will need much of the same equipment required for making soft cheese: a dairy thermometer; a room thermometer; a measuring jug; a 10–15 litre (2–3 gallon) bucket for making cheese; a spare bucket for collecting whey; cheese cloths; a teaspoon, tablespoon, or measuring spoons, long-handled spoon, long-bladed knife; starter bottles. In addition you will need:

A cheese mould and press You may be able to obtain a proper cheese press second-hand (see illustration opposite). Alternatively, you can improvise with a cake tin, wooden follower and weights (see illustration below).

Cake tin with holes pierced in the side.

Wooden follower.

An improvised cheese press.

A cheese press This takes the curd from 25–30 litres (6–7 gallons) of milk. It is not difficult to buy one new online and there are a number of small presses advertised for the small home producer.

You can improvise with two round plastic sweet tins of the kind you get at Christmas. Use one as your cheese mould; it will hold about 2–3kg (4½–6½lb). Drill holes in the bottom to allow the cheese to drain and use the other as the follower to sit on top and then you can put weights in it – building bricks or other similar weights can be used; the actual weight needed will depend on the variety of cheese being made. I was lucky enough to find a door weight of 13.6kg (30lb), which is ideal for pressing Smallholder cheese.

A bowl for collecting the whey as the cheese is pressed A small, shallow container in which the cheese mould can be placed will be sufficient, as most of the whey will have been released during previous processes.

Butter muslin for making the cheese bandage The cheese will keep better if it is bandaged with butter muslin (see 'cheese cloths' on page 31).

PREMISES

If you live on a farm you may have a scullery, large larder,
suitable outhouse or even a dairy that you can adapt into a special
cheesemaking room. However, if you have no other suitable room,
the kitchen will do well. The room chosen must first of all be
cleaned very thoroughly, and subsequently be kept very clean.
Contamination of the milk or curd could lead to serious defects in the
cheese (see page 26).

The room temperature should range from 18–21°C (65–70°F) to
obtain uniform drainage of the curd. Neither cold and damp nor hot,
dry rooms are suitable. The temperature can be regulated by window
ventilation and by the provision of some sort of heater.

There should be a sufficient area of level shelving and tables
or workbenches. Working surfaces should be washable and well
scrubbed, preferably stainless steel. Hooks can be fixed to the
underside of shelves for hanging the soft cheeses while draining.
Plenty of hot water should be available for the cleaning and
sterilization of all equipment used. In addition, if you are making
hard cheese, you will need a suitable place in which to store the
maturing cheese. This should maintain an even, cool temperature
of 10–16°C (50–60°F) and should not be too dry or too damp. It is
important it is also vermin proof.

CARE OF EQUIPMENT

It cannot be emphasized too many times that all utensils must be properly cleaned and sterilized each time they are used. Milk is an ideal medium for the growth of micro-organisms; inadequate cleaning and sterilization may lead to its contamination and the consequent spoilage of the cheese.

Immediately after use utensils should be rinsed and scrubbed thoroughly in cold water. If hot water is used first, a deposit of milk will be 'baked' onto the surface of the utensil. Next wash and scrub in hot soapy water. An ordinary kitchen liquid detergent or alternatively washing soda crystals can be used. Rinse thoroughly in clean hot water and complete with sterilization.

Sterilization

This can be achieved by:
- boiling in water
- steaming
- use of a hypochlorite sterilizing solution

A large saucepan with a fitted lid can be used for boiling or steaming. A galvanized clothes boiler is also suitable, but this can only be used on a gas stove because of its raised bottom. Either immerse the equipment completely in boiling water, or else place it in a pan with about 5cm (2in) of boiling water, replace the lid and steam for five minutes. Wooden boards, cloths and mats require special care for they can easily harbour contaminating organisms. Immerse them in boiling water for at least 20 minutes. Remember that you can boil or steam most plastic or polythene equipment.

Hypochlorite sterilizing solution can be used for much of the equipment and has the advantage that you are not enveloped in clouds of steam. Metal utensils other than stainless steel should not be put in the solution as they will corrode, but it is quite safe for cheese cloths and boards. Cheese cloths which have been stained by the cheese will regain their white colour.

If you live on a farm you may have dairy sterilizer available – use it according to the makers' instructions. Otherwise you can use Milton, which is available from chemists or at the baby section of large supermarkets.

Make up your solution in a plastic bucket into which the utensils can then be placed. Always rinse the utensils thoroughly afterwards with clean cold water to remove any traces of the hypochlorite which might otherwise interfere with the cheesemaking bacteria. Leave the utensils to drain dry, and store them carefully in a clean place. Immediately before use all equipment should be resterilized.

A dilute solution of hypochlorite can also be used for wiping down work surfaces and walls in the cheesemaking room.

INGREDIENTS

MILK

The milk used for cheesemaking should be of the highest hygienic quality. If you live on a dairy farm or keep a house cow or goat you will have a ready supply of raw milk available. To make sure that this milk is safe and free from contamination or disease-causing organisms, it is advisable to pasteurize it before use.

If you do not have your own supply of milk, and cannot obtain milk direct from a farm, use the milk delivered by your local milkman or from your local supermarket. It is perfectly suitable. Use pasteurized milk – not sterilized or ultra-heat-treated (UHT) milk for cheeses made with rennet; the temperatures used in sterilization and ultra-heat treatment are higher than the pasteurization temperature and so cause changes in the milk which affect rennet action (this is explained in the section on the principles of cheesemaking, see page 13–15).

Pasteurization of the milk

Pour the milk into a stainless-steel bucket (do not use a plastic bucket for this) and then place the bucket in a larger container filled with boiling water (see illustration opposite). Raise the temperature of the milk to 71°C (160°F) for 15 seconds, stirring occasionally to ensure even heating. This is the pasteurization temperature which will kill all the disease-causing organisms.

Cool at once to 4.5°C (40°F) by putting the bucket into cold running water and keep the milk at this temperature until used; remember that most bacteria like warm conditions for growth. The milk should be stirred carefully to prevent a skin forming while cooling, and then covered. You may find it quicker and easier to pasteurize smaller quantities at a time.

CREAM

Again if you live on a farm you will have a ready supply of cream available. The section on cream (see pages 123–128) gives details of how to separate and pasteurize this cream. If you buy your cream from a dairy or grocer use pasteurized single or double cream, depending upon the type of cream cheese you wish to make.

Bucket of milk.

Basin of
boiling water.

Pasteurizing the milk.

RENNET

Rennet comes in several forms:

Animal rennet is traditionally used for cheese production. It is extracted from the lining of calf's, kid's or lamb's stomachs.

Vegetarian rennet is more commonly used today, as it is cheaper and ethically more acceptable. The rennet is produced by culturing and extracting from moulds such as *Mucor mehei* and bacteria such as *Bacillus subtilis*. Modilase and Marzyme are two such brands available.

Plant rennets are not widely used – some plant extracts such as those from thistles, nettles and fig-tree bark can be used to clot milk, but this can be very hit and miss.

Chymosin is made by genetic modification of the calf chymosin gene (for example, Maxiren and Chy-max). This type of rennet is not approved by organic bodies for use in organic cheese production.

Once obtained, the rennet should be kept in a cool, dark place with the stopper tightly secured. Rennet is always measured out immediately before use. Junket rennet, which can be bought at most chemists and grocers, is much weaker than cheese rennet, but can be used as an alternative in some of the soft-cheese recipes. Cheese rennet is available in liquid form but junket rennet is now available as tablets. A tablet is ground into a powder and dissolved in cold water first, following the instructions on the packet.

Rennet activity deteriorates with time even if it is kept in the refrigerator. Before cheesemaking it is advisable to carry out a simple test to check whether the cheese rennet is still suitable for use. Add one drop of rennet from a medical or eye dropper to a dessertspoon of milk previously warmed to between 30 and 37°C (86 and 98°F). The milk should set within five minutes.

ANNATTO

Annatto is a natural vegetable colouring that can be used if required to give a reddish colour to the cheese. It comes from the outer coating of the seeds of *Bixa orellana*, a small tropical tree, and is also used to dye fabrics and butter among other things.

SALT

The addition of salt helps to preserve the cheese and also to bring out the flavour. Ordinary household salt can be used.

LARD

You will need a good-quality lard to coat semi-hard cheeses (see page 97).

Ingredients

CHEESE STARTER

Cheese starter is milk that contains a special bacterial culture; this is responsible for producing acid during the cheesemaking process and also contributes to the flavour of the cheese. The bacteria in cheese starter use the milk sugar – lactose – for growth, and change it into lactic acid. Most starters used in cheesemaking are controlled cultures of *Lactococcus lactis lactis*, *Lactococcus lactis cremoris* and *Lactococcus lactis diacetylactis*. These lactic bacteria produce lactic acid very rapidly.

Many of the cheeses in this book require cheese starter. There have been many scientific and technological advances over the last 40 years in the development of specific cultures for the dairy industry. One of the most significant is the introduction of DVI or Direct-to-Vat Innoculation. This has benefited large creameries and small home producers alike. A freeze-dried culture stored in the fridge or deep freeze can now be added to the milk in the cheese vat without the need to prepare and cultivate a culture beforehand (as described below).

Recultivation of starter

A newly bought starter will keep for up to three days in a refrigerator. If kept for longer it will deteriorate; the lactic bacteria stored in acid conditions even in the cold lose their viability. Starter can, however, be kept viable by recultivation. This involves the addition of a small amount of starter to fresh sterilized milk to form a new culture which will then grow strongly when kept in warm conditions. Recultivation should be carried out at frequent intervals to ensure that you always have a good, viable starter available. Ideally it should be done every day, but this may prove tedious and time-consuming to the amateur cheesemaker who only makes cheese once a week. So below a method is outlined in which starter can be recultivated just once a week.

Suitable bottles for cheese starter cultivation.

Heat treatment of starter bottles and milk First the bottles and milk used for recultivation must be heat treated. The best way to do this is to heat treat both at the same time, by heating the milk in the bottles. Use screw-cap glass bottles with a narrow neck. They should have a capacity of about 170ml (6fl oz), and should be heat resistant. Sauce bottles or children's orange-juice bottles are suitable (see illustration above). Before using them for the first time, wash the bottles very carefully and then immerse them in boiling water for 20 minutes; this will sterilize the bottles and at the same time serve as a test that they can withstand the heat.

You can make up two bottles of culture at a time; one can be used for cheesemaking and the other for recultivation. Pour 140ml (5fl oz) of milk into each bottle and screw the caps on loosely. This is to allow the hot air to escape as the bottles heat up, and to re-enter as the bottles cool; if you screw the caps on too tightly, watch out for exploding bottles! Place the bottles in a saucepan with 2.5–5cm

(1–2in) of water in the bottom. If you have or can make a suitable bottle rack this will prevent the bottles from moving around. Otherwise you can improvise by wedging the bottles with jam jars half full of water, or with other suitable objects (see illustration below).

Place the lid on the pan and heat. For adequate sterilization the water should boil continuously for 30 minutes. Remove the bottles and cool until just lukewarm to the touch; do not plunge the hot bottles straight into cold water.

Jam jar half filled with water.

Starter bottle filled with milk.

Sterilizing the milk and bottles for the starter.

A pressure cooker can also be used. Cover the bottom plate with at least 2.5cm (1in) of water. Hold the bottles at 1 bar (15psi) for ten minutes. Leave to depressurize for at least 10 minutes and then cool the bottles.

Transfer of starter You are now ready to transfer the starter to the new bottles. To help prevent contamination this should be done in an upward current of air, for example in the steam over a saucepan of boiling water (see illustration below) – but take care not to scald yourself. Add ½ teaspoon of starter culture to each bottle of milk, and screw the caps down fully. Shake well. Throw away the remaining contents of the old bottle of starter.

Transferring the starter into the culture bottles.

If proper care is taken, the above method of starter transfer works very well for those with limited facilities. However the best way to protect your starter against contamination is to use the Lewis method. This involves the use of polythene bottles fitted with special rubber seals. The starter is transferred by piercing the rubber seals with a double-ended inoculating needle, and gently squeezing the bottles. The starter bottles remain airtight throughout the process, and as a result there is little chance of any contamination. The equipment needed, with full instructions for use, can be bought online, but it is relatively expensive and the procedure a little more complicated for the small home cheesemaker. However you may consider it worth the investment.

If, having transferred the starter, you only wish to recultivate it once a week, do not incubate it at once but place the bottle(s) in the refrigerator; the starter will keep there for up to a week without deteriorating. The number of bacteria present at this stage is small, and will not produce enough acid to kill the culture.

If you wish to make cheese the next day you can incubate the culture for this immediately.

Incubation of starter When needed, the starter culture should be incubated in a warm place for 12 hours or until the milk coagulates. Ideally cheese starter should be incubated at 22°C (72°F), but a temperature between 21 and 27°C (70 and 80°F) is satisfactory.

Incubators

The linen cupboard A linen cupboard that maintains a steady temperature is very suitable; check this with a room thermometer. Its disadvantage is that you may not wish to mix your linen with your cheese!

A baby's bottle warmer This usually has a selection of temperature settings; you can find the right one by placing a bottle containing water and a thermometer in the warmer and reading the temperature the water finally reaches at each setting. (I find, with my bottle warmer, that the right temperature is reached when the warmer is just switched on – below setting no. 1.) Only one bottle can be incubated at a time.

An improvised wooden box incubator A small wooden box with a light bulb can be rigged up as an incubator (see illustration opposite). The size of the box is not important, but the wattage of the light bulb used for heating should be increased or decreased accordingly. To find the right bulb for your box, experiment with different bulbs until the correct temperature is maintained – check this with a thermometer inside the box. (For example, my incubator consists of a modified orange box with a 15-watt bulb.)

The box can be refined further by the addition of inner walls of Formica which can be easily cleaned; and in between these and the outer wooden walls a layer of insulating material such as cotton wool or polystyrene can be inserted to prevent changes in temperature.

This box incubator can also be used to sour milk and cream to make lactic and cream cheese, to ripen cream for butter-making, and to incubate cultured buttermilk and yoghurt culture. Yoghurt culture requires a higher temperature – 43°C (110°F) – and so a more

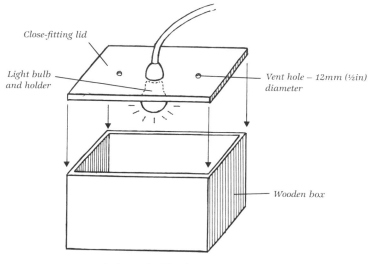

Close-fitting lid

Light bulb and holder

Vent hole – 12mm (½in) diameter

Wooden box

An improvised incubator.

powerful light bulb should be fitted for this. If you wish to incubate larger quantities you can use a larger wooden box.

When the milk in the culture bottle has coagulated, place the culture in a refrigerator until needed for cheesemaking or recultivation later that day. On shaking the coagulated milk, the culture should have a fairly thick but still runny, smooth consistency, similar to a runny yoghurt. After use the bottles should be well washed and sterilized; a bottle brush or teapot-spout brush will help to clean them thoroughly.

If the procedure for starter cultivation seems unduly complicated, the chart on page 57 may help to make it clearer.

Note You may find that over time the culture becomes weakened and will not set the milk firmly when incubated. If so, throw this away and buy a new culture. It is most important to have a good starter. Remember that a viable starter should give a firm set within 12 hours of the milk being incubated.

An alternative method of starter cultivation using the deep freeze

If you have a deep freeze you can make up a larger number of culture bottles at one time from your initial culture, and then store them in the freezer for up to three months. The bottles of culture can be taken out and used as and when required. This prevents contamination as a result of continuous recultivation, and also saves the time and effort needed each week to recultivate the starter.

Use 120ml (4fl oz) polythene bottles, not glass ones; sterilize the milk and bottles, and transfer the starter as described on page 52. Add just under ½ teaspoon of starter culture to the 120ml (4fl oz) of milk in each bottle and place in the freezer within 20 minutes. When you take a bottle out of the freezer, place it first in hot water at 29°C (85°F) for 2 hours; this helps to bring it up to the right temperature. Then incubate at 21–27°C (70–80°F) for 12 hours as before.

A SUGGESTED PROGRAMME FOR STARTER CULTIVATION FOR THOSE WHO WISH TO MAKE CHEESE ABOUT ONCE A WEEK

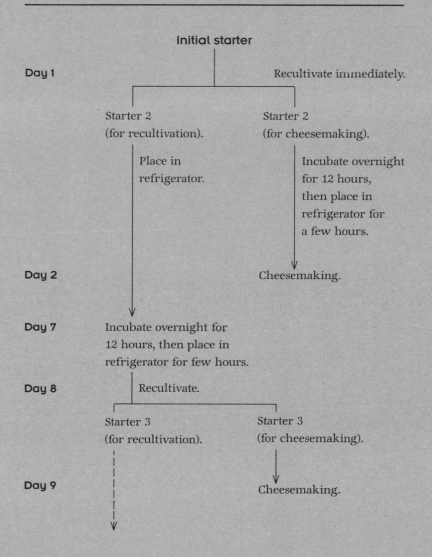

Initial starter

Day 1   Recultivate immediately.

Starter 2 (for recultivation).

Starter 2 (for cheesemaking).

Place in refrigerator.

Incubate overnight for 12 hours, then place in refrigerator for a few hours.

Day 2   Cheesemaking.

Day 7   Incubate overnight for 12 hours, then place in refrigerator for few hours.

Day 8   Recultivate.

Starter 3 (for recultivation).

Starter 3 (for cheesemaking).

Day 9   Cheesemaking.

Supply of cheese starter

As mentioned earlier, you can obtain cheese starter by post, either in liquid form or as a freeze-dried culture. The latter has the advantage that it will keep practically indefinitely until opened, but then it must be used at once. The freeze-dried culture is reactivated when added to sterilized milk and incubated; it can be recultivated in the same way as the liquid culture.

The instructions with the freeze-dried culture may suggest the use of 1–2 pints of milk for the first cultivation, but these have been written for the commercial cheesemaker who needs a large quantity. You can instead use two bottles each containing 140ml (5fl oz) as before, and add half the contents of your bottle of freeze-dried culture to each one. If you intend to use the deep freeze, recultivate the freeze-dried culture in the ordinary way twice to make sure that the culture is working well, before making up the larger number of bottles for the deep freeze.

A warning to those with a supply of milk direct from a dairy farm
Starter activity can be inhibited by the presence of antibiotics in the milk. Antibiotics are used in the treatment of mastitis and may be present in the milk for some days after treatment has ceased. The milk from treated cows should therefore not be used for cheesemaking for about 2–3 days until the excretion of antibiotics has stopped. This, however, does not apply to those who buy milk from a dairy, since this milk has been bulked from many different farms and it is rare for it to contain inhibitory quantities of antibiotics.

MAKING

SOFT

CHEESE

A note on using goat's milk

The recipes in this book have been developed with cow's milk, but goat's milk can also be used. The fat globules in goat's milk are smaller, however, and this influences the temperatures needed for some of the recipes. Renneting temperatures, for example, are lower. Where there is a difference, the relevant temperatures for goat's milk have been indicated.

Bowl and muslin-lined colander.

FRESH MILK CHEESE

If you have never made cheese before, this very simple cheese is a good one to make first and will demonstrate some of the basic principles involved.

First set a litre (¾ pint) of milk by heating the milk in a double saucepan or in a bowl standing in a saucepan of simmering water, until it reaches 38°C (100°F). Check the temperature with your thermometer. Remove the top saucepan or bowl from the hot water. Dissolve a junket rennet tablet in cold water and add it to the warm milk. Stir well. Cover the bowl and leave in a warm place for two hours until the junket has set.

Next, line a colander with a square of muslin. Stand the colander in a bowl (see illustration above). Ladle thin slices of curd into the muslin. You will notice that as you slice into the curd a watery liquid appears; this is the whey. As the whey runs into the bowl underneath and the curd sinks in the colander, add more curd until you have used it all.

Gather the corners of the cloth together and tie a piece of string tightly round it to make a bag. Hang it on a hook with a bowl underneath to catch the whey (see illustration opposite). Leave it to drain for 1–2 hours.

The curd in its bag is now ready to be placed in a soft-cheese mould – a Coulommiers hoop or an improvised mould (see page 32). First place the mould on a cheese board, and then place this in a pan to catch the whey (see illustration on page 73). Put the bag of curd into the mould and leave it for several hours so that the curd takes the shape of the mould. Remember to save the whey. After this the cheese can be carefully removed from the muslin. Wrap it in greaseproof paper and keep it in the refrigerator. It should be eaten within 2–3 days. One litre of milk will make about 225–300g (8–10oz) of cheese; it has a bland taste and a smooth texture.

Fresh milk cheese can be eaten in a variety of ways. It is traditionally served swimming in a flat dish of whey, as curds and whey. Pour fresh cream over the top and sprinkle it with caster sugar. Alternatively, the solid curd can be eaten with soft or stewed fruit. The whey is a refreshing drink when served cold; it can also be used for mixing scones or cakes. To make a savoury cheese, sprinkle salt on both sides of the curd. You can then press dried herbs such as savory, oregano, marjoram or thyme into each side of the curd, or roll it in fine oatmeal.

Bag of curd draining.

ACID-CURD CHEESES (DRAIN CURD)

These cheeses are formed by the action of acid on the milk protein (see page 24) and are very easy to make. The simplest of all is a lemon cheese made with lemon juice. Although it is not a true cheese its manufacture will illustrate the principles involved in making an acid-curd cheese.

Lemon cheese

Heat 1 litre (1¾ pints) of milk to 38°C (100°F) in a double saucepan or a bowl standing in a saucepan of simmering water. Remove the bowl from the hot water. Add the juice of two lemons to the milk and stir well. Leave for 15 minutes. You will notice that the milk immediately separates into rather stringy curds and whey.

Line a colander with muslin as for the fresh milk cheese (see page 63). Ladle the curd into the muslin with a perforated ladle or spoon. Now gather the corners of the cloth together and tie with a piece of string. Hang the bag over a bowl and leave for one hour to drain. Remove the cheese from the muslin; you may have to scrape it off the sides with a knife. Add about ¼ teaspoon salt to taste.

The cheese is now ready to eat. One litre of milk makes 225–300g (8–10oz) of cheese. It has a moist, spreadable texture and a very pleasant, slightly lemon taste. The whey can be used in baking or served as a nutritious cold drink.

Cultured buttermilk cheese

Cultured buttermilk contains a bacterial culture similar to that in a cheese starter. For this cheese you can either buy 600ml (1 pint) of fresh cultured buttermilk from your local dairy or grocer, or else make your own as described in the section on buttermilk (see page 132). The culture in the buttermilk means that it has already coagulated into a thick consistency.

Pour the buttermilk into a double saucepan or bowl and heat slowly over water to 71°C (160°F), stirring occasionally. The heat will cause the curd to separate. Remove the bowl from the hot water, cover it and leave it for about two hours to allow the curd to settle.

Line a colander with muslin as before and tip the contents of the bowl into the muslin. Tie the muslin bag, hang it over a bowl and leave it to drain for two hours. Remove the cheese from the muslin, scraping it off the sides if necessary, and add salt to taste. 600ml (1 pint) of buttermilk will make 120–140g (4–5oz) of cheese; it has a granular, spreadable texture and a slightly acid taste.

If you want a very moist cheese, only heat the buttermilk to 38°C (100°F). A shorter draining time also gives a moister cheese, and you can experiment to obtain a result to suit your personal taste.

Yoghurt cheese

Yoghurt makes a similar soft cheese. Use fresh natural yoghurt; to buy 600ml (1 pint) of yoghurt is relatively expensive, so it is more economical to make your own as described on pages 118–121.

Heat the yoghurt in a double saucepan to 38°C (100°F) and then pour it into the muslin. Hang up the muslin bag and leave it to drain for several hours in the usual way. Remove the cheese from the muslin and add salt to taste.

This is a moist cheese with a slight acid, yoghurt flavour.

Lactic cheese

In the past this cheese was often made from raw milk that had soured. Now most milk sold is pasteurized, and even if you have your own supply of milk direct from the cow it is still advisable to pasteurize it. Remember it is not safe to use pasteurized milk that has gone off for cheesemaking (see page 24), and cheese starter should be used to sour the milk. You can use whole or skimmed milk.

Heat the milk to 24°C (75°F) and add 15ml (1 tablespoon) of mesophilic starter MA4001 to one litre of milk. A better set is obtained if you boil the milk first for one minute and then cool it to 24°C (75°F) before adding the starter. You will have to boil the milk directly in a saucepan since it is difficult to raise it to boiling point in a bowl over water. Cover the bowl and leave it in a warm place – 21–27°C (70–80°F) – for 12 hours or until the milk has coagulated – it is important to maintain the temperature until the curd sets. A soup kettle or a wooden box incubator are suitable places (see the section on starter cultivation, page 54).

Pour the coagulated milk into a muslin and leave it to drain as before. Add salt to taste. If you are using larger quantities of milk you will find that drainage will take longer – up to two or three days. Drainage can be hastened by opening the cloth at intervals, scraping down the curd on the outside of the cloth and mixing it well with the softer curd in the middle. The cloth can also be changed at intervals.

Packaging

These cheeses are of a fairly runny consistency and you will find it easier to pack them in firm containers. Small polythene containers with lids are excellent, or otherwise you can save old yoghurt and cream cartons. Wash them well and dip them in hypochlorite solution before use to sterilize them properly. Rinse well. When the cheeses have been packed they can be covered with tinfoil. Keep the cheeses in a cool place or refrigerator, and eat within two to three days.

TRUE SOFT CHEESES
(LACTIC-FORMED CHEESE)

True soft cheeses are made with rennet, although their clean acid flavour is also due to the addition of a bacterial starter culture. Most are made in traditional moulds of a particular shape and size.

Crowdie (or cottage cheese)

Similar to American Bakers' cheese, Crowdie is an old-fashioned Scottish cottage cheese. It is traditionally made from skimmed or separated milk, but you can use whole fat milk.

Heat 1.13 litres (2 pints) of milk to 90°F (32°C); for goat's milk use 29°C (85°F).

Add 30ml (2 tablespoons) of cheese starter MA4001 (alternatively you can dilute ¼ teaspoon (1ml) of cheese rennet in six times its own volume of cool, boiled water). Stir well. Cover the bowl and leave in a warm place for about two hours.

When the curd has set, cut it into 2.5cm (1in) cubes with a long knife; cut it vertically and then turn the curd over carefully with a spoon and cut it the other way. Now heat the curd to 32°C (90°F), stirring it all the time, and leave it to settle for 10 minutes. Ladle the curd into a muslin and hang it up to drain for several hours.

Remove the cheese from the muslin and add salt. If a slightly richer cheese is required, some single cream can be added and mixed thoroughly with the curd. It can then be patted into a rectangular shape and pressed lightly with a cheese board. Wrap it in greaseproof paper, store in the refrigerator and eat within 2–3 days.

Coulommiers cheese

The traditional moulds used for Coulommiers cheese are made
in two parts, with one hoop fitting into the other (see illustration
below). They are so designed that the top section can be removed
when the curd has sunk to the level of the bottom one. The moulds
are 10–13cm (4–5in) in diameter and 13–15cm (5–6in) high when
fitted together. If you do not have the proper moulds then coffee or
cocoa tins can be used, as shown on page 32. Choose tins that are
about the same size as the complete Coulommiers mould, and cut
out their base. 4.5 litres (1 gallon) of milk will make three cheeses
about 10cm (4in) in diameter and 4cm (1½in) high. If you use
2.3 litres (4 pints) of milk you can make two slightly smaller
cheeses, but remember that all the other ingredients will have
to be adjusted in proportion.

Coulommiers moulds.

Renneting Heat the milk to 32°C (90°F); for goat's milk heat to 29°C (85°F). The best way to do this is to place the bucket or bowl of milk in a sink of hot water and stir the milk until the correct temperature is reached. Remove the bucket from the hot water, and add ½ teaspoon mesophilic starter (MA4001) to each gallon of milk, stirring well. Then measure out 5ml (1 teaspoon) of cheese rennet to every 4.5 litres (1 gallon) of milk, and dilute this with six times its own volume of cool, boiled water to ensure thorough mixing (i.e. 1 teaspoon of rennet and 6 teaspoons of water). Add the diluted rennet to the milk and stir in well. Then 'topstir' for about 10 minutes until the milk coagulates. This involves stirring the top 5mm (¼in) of the milk very smoothly and firmly to prevent the fat from rising to the surface. You can tell when coagulation is beginning because the curd will tend to cling to your stirrer as you take it out of the milk. Cover the container and leave for one hour or until the curd is firm. To test this, push a finger into the curd and out again – if the curd is ready it will split cleanly with a firm edge.

Preparing the moulds Meanwhile sterilize the moulds, straw mats and cheese boards by boiling them or by using a hypochlorite solution (see page 39). Place the moulds on a straw mat and board and stand all this in a shallow pan (see illustration below). If you cannot obtain suitable straw mats, you can use a folded cheese cloth, but make sure that it overhangs the edge of the cheese board slightly to facilitate drainage.

The mould standing on a mat and cheese board in a shallow pan.

Filling the moulds First skim off 'tops', which are used later to give a level surface to the cheese: press a mould down on top of the curd, then very carefully scoop out this piece of curd and slide it onto a clean plate or saucer. Cut one top for each mould. Next carefully ladle thin slices of curd and place them evenly in the moulds, lowering the ladle right to the bottom of the mould and letting the curd slip gently into place (see illustration opposite). It is best to fill all the moulds at the same time so that the curd is evenly distributed between them and you will finish with cheeses of the same size. Try to avoid breaking the curd, as this will result in a loss of fat and a tough, dry cheese.

The curd's rate of drainage is influenced by the thickness of the layers – thin slices will increase it and thick ones decrease it. If the slices of curd are too thick the whey will drain too slowly. The temperature is important too – if too much heat is lost, the whey will not drain quickly enough and the curd will not sink in the mould. Try to maintain as even a temperature as possible in your cheesemaking room: 16–21°C (60–70°F) is ideal.

Go on filling the moulds until the curd reaches the top, then leave for a few minutes until it sinks down a little in the moulds; ladle in more curd until you have used it all. Now slide on the 'tops'. Be careful not to knock the moulds or you will find that the curd shoots out.

Ladling the curd into the mould.

Turning the mould on to a new mat and board.

Draining and turning Leave the moulds to drain in a warm place until the curd has sunk below the level of the top hoop (about 24 hours). The top hoop can then be removed and the cheese turned onto a new, freshly sterilized mat and board. The best way to do this is to place the new mat and board on top of the moulds and, holding both boards between your hands, turn them over quickly. Then take away the old board and carefully remove the mat, so that the cheese comes away free and does not stick to it (see illustration opposite).

If you do not have the double moulds and so cannot remove a top section, take great care with the turning as the cheese will fall some distance from the top to the bottom of the mould and can easily be damaged or spoilt. Remember to clean and sterilize the old mat and board immediately after use.

Continue to turn the cheeses onto fresh mats and boards every 24 hours until they are firm. By the third day the curd should have drained enough to leave the sides of the moulds. Remove the moulds and rub about 15g (2 tablespoons) of salt into the surface of each cheese.

If the cheeses require further firming they can be drained out of the mould and turned every day, but at this stage must be kept in a cool, dry atmosphere. The surface of the cheese may become mouldy; if so wipe off any mould with a damp cloth dipped in cold water and put the cheese in a colder, drier place.

The cheese can be eaten immediately but will be found to improve if kept in a refrigerator or cool place for a couple of days. Lightly wrap in greaseproof paper and eat within a week.

Colwick cheese

Colwick is an English soft cheese and was traditionally made in a single perforated cylindrical mould about 18cm (7in) high and 13cm (5in) in diameter. However the moulds are no longer available and Coulommiers moulds can be used instead. The top hoop will not be removed since the cheese is not turned. If improvised moulds are used, the base of the tin should be cut away and holes pierced in the sides. 4.5 litres (1 gallon) of milk will make two cheeses; 2.3 litres (4 pints) will make one cheese.

Renneting Heat the milk to 32°C (90°F) for cow's milk, 29°C (85°F) for goat's milk. Add ½ teaspoon of mesophilic cheese starter (MA4001)and 1ml (1 small teaspoon) of cheese rennet (diluted with six times its own volume of water) to each 4.5 litres (1 gallon) of milk; stir in well. Topstir for about 10 minutes until coagulation begins (see page 72), then cover the container and leave for 1–1½ hours until the curd is firm.

Preparing the moulds Set up the moulds on the straw mat and cheese board in a shallow pan as before (see page 73), but this time line each mould with a cheesecloth that is large enough to fold over the top of the curd.

Filling the moulds and draining Slice off two 'tops' and place them in clean saucers. Ladle the curd in thin slices into the moulds as described on page 74, leave to drain a little and slide on the tops. Leave to drain for an hour, then pull the muslin upwards and inwards so that the curd is pulled away from the sides of the mould. This produces the characteristic curling over of the edge of Colwick cheese.

Repeat at intervals during the next four hours. The cheese is not turned; allow it to drain for 24–36 hours when it should be firm enough to handle. Remove the mould and pull the muslin very carefully away from the cheese.

The cheese is now ready to eat, but should be stored in a refrigerator if not eaten immediately. It can be salted, but traditionally it is not, and is served either as a sweet or a savoury. The hollow in the centre can be filled with whipped cream.

Cambridge or York cheese

This is another English soft cheese which used to be made around the Isle of Ely and was sold in the markets of Cambridge. The traditional moulds were rectangular and made in two parts; the top portion was about 18–20cm (7–8in) long, 10–13cm (4–5in) wide and 15cm (6in) deep, and was placed in a shallow tray holding a fitted piece of straw mat. The cheese was served on its straw mat. These moulds are available from cheesemaking suppliers online.

6.8 litres (1½ gallons) of milk will make two cheeses weighing 340–450g (¾–1lb) each; 3.4 litres (6 pints) will make one cheese. Cambridge cheese is not salted and has a coloured stripe running through the middle.

Renneting Heat the milk to 32°C (90°F); for goat's milk use 29°C (85°F). To each 6.8 litres (1½ gallons) of milk add 1 teaspoon of mesophilic cheese starter (MA4001) and 1 teaspoon of cheese rennet diluted in water. Stir in well for a minute or two and then if you want a coloured stripe in the middle of your cheese remove 2–3 litres (4 pints) from each 6.8 litres (1½ gallons) of milk and place in another container (in other words, remove a third of the mixture). To this add 1 teaspoon (2–3ml) of annatto and stir in until the colour is uniform. Do not topstir the remaining milk, as this cheese has a creamy top. Cover both containers and leave for 1–1½ hours until firm and the curd splits cleanly over the finger (see page 72).

Filling the moulds and draining Sterilize the moulds, a straw mat or cheese cloth and a board and set up as before (see illustration on page 73). Slice off the creamy tops by pressing a mould on top of the uncoloured curd where the cream has risen and skimming off carefully. Place the tops on clean plates. Then ladle thin layers of curd into the moulds; first ladle out about two-thirds of the plain, uncoloured curd, then all the coloured curd, and finish off with the remaining uncoloured curd before positioning the tops. You will find that when drainage is complete the coloured stripe will be roughly in the centre of the cheese.

Leave the curd to drain in the moulds for 2–3 days. Do not turn or add any salt. When the cheese is firm enough the moulds can be removed and the cheeses carefully lifted from the mat. They are now ready to eat and should be stored in a cool place. If mould begins to develop on the cheese surface, it should be wiped off; further mould growth can be prevented by leaving a clean piece of blotting paper on the surface to soak up the whey until the cheese is eaten.

Traditionally this cheese is cut into three portions for serving. It has a sharp, cleanly acid flavour.

A FEW FAVOURITE CHEESES.

1. Parmesan
2. Stilton.
3. Gruyere
4. Bondon
5. Dutch

6. Camembert
7. Roquefort
8. Neufchatel
9. Cheshire
10. Gorgonzola.

11. Cream
12. Devonshire Toasting Cheese
13. Cheddar.
14. Single Gloucester
15. Blue Dorset.

CREAM CHEESES

Cream cheeses are traditionally moulded into small cylindrical, square or rectangular shapes of various sizes and weights. Unfortunately the small metal moulds are no longer available, though you can buy plastic versions in a limited number of sizes, and you can improvise in various ways as described below.

Single cream cheese

This is made from single cream as its name suggests, and needs rennet for coagulation. Single cream has a butterfat content of 18–25 per cent.

Heat 1 litre (1¾ pints) of single cream to 24°C (75°F). Add 1 teaspoon of mesophilic cheese starter (MA4001) and mix well. Cover the bowl and leave in a warm place for 2–3 hours to allow the cream to ripen. Alternatively you can use freshly bought soured cream. Do not use pasteurized cream that has gone sour. Warm the soured cream to 24°C (75°F).

Next dilute ¼ teaspoon (0.5ml) of rennet with six times its own volume of cold boiled water, and add this to the cream, stirring well to mix. Cover the bowl and leave in a warm place or incubator at 21–27°C (70–80°F) for 8–12 hours or until the cream coagulates (see the section on starter cultivation, pages 53–57).

Ladle the coagulum in slices into a thick cloth (two cheese cloths put together work very well). Hang it up to drain in a cool, well-ventilated room – 10–13°C (50–55°F). Alternatively, the bag of curd can be placed horizontally between two cheese boards with a 450–900g (1–2lb) weight on top. The boards can then be placed in a tin to collect the whey. This hastens the draining process.

During the draining period the cloth should be opened at 4–8 hourly intervals and the curd on the outside near the cloth scraped down and mixed well with the softer curd in the middle. The more often this is done the quicker the curd will drain. If the cloth becomes clogged with curd drainage will be restricted. The cloth should be changed at intervals. When sufficiently drained the curd will have a thick, rather granular consistency. Add salt and mix well.

The cheese can be shaped into a round pat and wrapped in greaseproof paper or tinfoil, or packed into plastic cartons. Keep it in the refrigerator and eat within 2–3 days.

Double-cream cheese

Double cream drains without rennet, but the addition of starter results in quicker drainage and a pleasant, slightly acid flavour to the cheese. It also improves its keeping quality. Double cream has a butterfat content of 48–55 per cent.

Heat 1 litre (1¾ pints) of double cream to 75°F (24°C); add as for single cream ½ teaspoon of mesophilic cheese starter and 5g (¼oz) of salt and stir well. Salting the cream at this stage helps it to drain well and improves its keeping quality. Cover the cream and leave it in a warm place to coagulate as before. Ladle it into a thick cloth and hang it up to drain in a cool place. Then treat as for single cream cheese.

WHEY CHEESES

When making cheese you will find that you have large quantities of whey left over. Do collect this – it can be used in baking or served as a cool refreshing drink. You can also try making whey cheeses.

Whey cheese

You will need 1.2 litres (2 pints) of milk to every 600ml (1 pint) of whey. Pour the whey directly into a saucepan and heat very slowly until bubbles begin to appear, then pour in the fresh milk. Continue heating for about ten minutes, stirring occasionally. Do not let the liquid boil. You will notice that the curd begins to separate. Take it off the heat, and cover the pan. Leave it for two hours to allow the curd to settle, then pour it into muslin. Hang up the muslin bag and drain for 2–3 hours. Add salt to taste, then pack it into plastic or polythene containers. Keep the cheese in a refrigerator and eat within 2–3 days.

Mysost cheese

Pour the whey into a saucepan and heat very slowly until the whey has evaporated to a thick treacle. This will take several hours. Then cool it rapidly by standing the pan in cold water. When cool the cheese should be the colour of honey, and have the consistency of butter. Pack it in small glass jars and seal tightly. 1.2 litres (2 pints) of whey will make about 120g (4oz) of cheese.

This cheese has a very strong smell and flavour, and you may find it an acquired taste!

MAKING

SEMI-HARD

CHEESE

SEMI-HARD CHEESE

Hard cheeses are not easy to make in the home because of the difficulty of applying enough pressure to press them really hard. However, with improvised moulds and weights, it is possible to make a semi-hard cheese. This requires a little more time and skill than soft cheese, but you will find there is a great sense of achievement in producing your own 'hard' cheese.

The importance of having acidity developing at a steady rate throughout the cheesemaking process has already been discussed in the section on the principles of cheesemaking (see pages 13–15). The commercial cheesemaker can measure the acidity at various stages by carrying out acidity tests. Kits are available to the small home cheesemaker, but the development of acidity can be judged by physical changes in the curd. These are explained in the recipes and will be learned with experience.

You will need to put aside a whole day (especially the first time) and have no other commitments since the cheese will need your attention for much of the time, and the process should not be hurried or interrupted.

The quantity of milk involved is somewhat larger than that required for soft cheese so remember to place an order with your milkman. If you live on a dairy farm or have your own cow or goat it is best to mix milk from the morning and evening milkings in equal proportions; evening milk is richer in fat than morning milk, and a mixture of the two milkings will result in a milk with a better fat content for hard cheesemaking. A high-fat milk gives a particularly soft velvety curd.

All the recipes in this section use 10 litres (2.2 gallons) of milk because this amount is convenient to handle in a 10–12 litre (2–2½ gallon) bucket. The 15cm (6in) cake tin mould (see illustration on page 32) will just take the curd from 10 litres (2 gallons) of milk, and 10 litres (2 gallons) will make about 900g (2lb) of cheese. If you have larger milk containers and a larger cheese mould and press you can use more milk, but remember to adjust all the other quantities in proportion.

A Smallholder cheese is a good one to try first. Each stage is described in detail. Once you have mastered this you can try one of the other recipes. You will see that the same processes are involved for each type of cheese; only the times and temperatures are different to give the variety in flavour and texture. The Caerphilly-type and Small Cheshire contain more moisture and less acidity than their larger sized namesakes.

Before you start, gather together all the equipment necessary and sterilize it.

SMALLHOLDER CHEESE
(AMERICAN FARM CHEESE)

Ripening Pour 10 litres (2.2 gallons) milk into a suitable bucket and heat to 32°C (90°F), or for goat's milk 29°C (85°F). This can be done by placing the bucket in a sink of hot water and stirring the milk until the correct temperature is reached. Then take the bucket out of the hot water, otherwise the temperature of the milk will continue to rise. Add 4 tablespoons of cheese starter and stir in well. Cover the bucket with a cheese cloth and leave for 45 minutes.

Renneting Use cheese rennet only. You need 2.5–3ml (1 teaspoon) of rennet for each 10 litres (2.2 gallons) of milk. Dilute it with three times its own volume of cold boiled water; this should be measured immediately before use. Check that the temperature of the milk is still 32°C (90°F), or for goat's milk 29°C (85°F), and if necessary bring it back to this temperature by replacing the bucket in the sink of hot water. Pour the diluted rennet carefully into the milk, and stir at once right down to the bottom of the bucket for half a minute. Then topstir (see page 72) until coagulation begins. Ideally this should take 10–15 minutes. You will be able to tell when coagulation is near because the curd feels dense and the bubbles stay on the surface instead of breaking.

The time that the rennet takes to coagulate the milk is an indication of the rate of acid development. If the milk sets in 10–15 minutes the acidity is developing at a good, steady rate. If the milk sets in less than 10 minutes then the acidity is developing fast; this may happen because the starter is very vigorous, the milk is dirty or the weather hot. If the milk takes longer than 15 minutes to set, then acidity is developing slowly, perhaps because the starter is not very active. High or low acid development can result in spoilt cheese. However, by adjusting the degree and length of scalding (see

page 19), it is possible to keep pace with the development of acidity, and so save your cheese.

When the milk has coagulated, cover the bucket and leave for about 45 minutes or until the curd is firm enough to split cleanly over your finger – again this time will depend on the rate of acid development. If the milk is left too long the whey will begin to separate out in pools on the surface of the curd.

Cutting the curd Both this stage and the scalding stage that comes next are a vital part of cheesemaking, and should not be hurried. The cutting and scalding allow the whey to drain from the curd particles. If the drainage happens too quickly the curd will become tough and the cheese will be leathery. Carefully cut the curd into 6–12mm (¼–½in) cubes. Make the first cuts with an ordinary stainless steel carving knife; holding it vertically, cut down and across the curd in one direction and then down and across it at right angles to the first cuts (see illustration opposite, top). Then, following the lines of these vertical cuts, cut the curd at an angle, diagonally, first in one direction and then in the other (see illustration opposite, bottom). Turn the curd over carefully in the bucket and stir it gently for about 5 minutes. Check that all the curd pieces are fairly even and cut up those that are too big.

Scalding The curd is now ready for scalding. Again, stand your bucket in a sink of hot water, and take about 30 minutes to heat the curd slowly and steadily to 38°C (100°F), or for goat's milk 35°C (95°F). Stir gently all the time to prevent the curd pieces from sticking together. It is generally better to heat the curd slowly at first, and then accelerate towards the end. You will notice that the curd pieces shrink in size and become firmer – when you scoop them up in your hand they should be firm enough to separate easily. To ensure that they are properly firm you can keep the curds and whey at 38°C (100°F) for a longer time (still stirring) until they separate even when squeezed in the hand.

If there has been an indication during renneting that the acidity is developing fast the curd must be drained of whey more quickly. This is done by scalding it to a higher temperature in a shorter time – for example, 41°C (105°F) in 20 minutes. If the curd is 'working slowly', slow scalding to a lower temperature – for example, 37°C (98°F) in 40 minutes) will result in slower drainage of whey. In either case the curd pieces should become firm and resilient, and separate easily when held or squeezed in the hand.

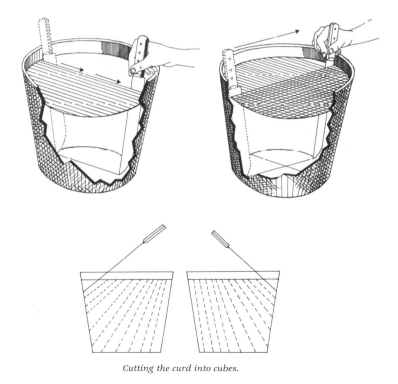

Cutting the curd into cubes.

Draining the whey Allow the curd to settle for a few minutes before draining. To drain the whey, tie a cloth over a spare bucket and then very gently tip the contents of the first bucket onto the cloth, so that the whey goes into the bucket and the curd remains in the cloth (see illustration below). You may find it easier to do this with two people. Afterwards tie up the corners of the cloth and make a bundle of the curd, put it back in the empty bucket and leave it to consolidate for about an hour, tightening the muslin every ten minutes or so to expel more whey (see illustration opposite). The curd should now have a rubbery texture and should make a squeaky sound when a small piece is chewed.

Pouring off the whey into a spare bucket.

Making Semi-hard Cheese

The curd wrapped in a tight bundle.

Salting Break the curd up cleanly into small pieces the size of a walnut, taking care not to squeeze out any fat. Turn the pieces over several times to allow them to cool and drain. Sprinkle on salt at a ratio of 20g (1½ tablespoons) to 10 litres (2 gallons) of milk – and mix it in well.

Moulding and pressing the curd Line your mould with a damp cheese cloth and pack in the curd as evenly as possible. Place smaller pieces of curd in the mould first, pack in the rest of the curd, and then finish off with small pieces; this will give a better finish to the top and bottom of the cheese. Fold the cheese cloth over the curd, and place the wooden follower on top of this. Put weights up to 13kg (28lb) on top. Remember to stand the mould in a pan to collect the whey.

After a few hours take the cheese out of the press and turn it. Wrap it in a dry cloth, and then put it back into the mould under increased pressure – up to 18kg (40lb) if possible. The next day turn the cheese again, using a new cloth, and place it back in the mould under as much weight as possible. Leave for 24 hours.

Finishing the cheese The simplest way to do this is to melt some lard and coat the surface of the cheese with a very thin layer. For a 1kg (2lb) cheese you will need 30–60g (1–2oz) of lard.

The cheese will keep better if it is bandaged as well. Cut some pieces of butter muslin – two round pieces slightly wider than the cheese for the top and the bottom, and one long piece to go round the cheese. Lay the muslin flat on the top and bottom, smoothing it down well; then wrap the long piece around, pulling the edges together to exclude the air (see illustration below). If you do not bandage the cheese, the outside surface should be rubbed over at intervals with a clean cloth to stop the development of mould.

Bandaging the cheese.

Maturing the cheese The cheese can be left to mature for 6–8 weeks before it is ready for eating; it will than have a firm body and a mild flavour. Store it in a cool place, neither too dry nor too damp, and which maintains an even temperature of 10–16°C (50–60°F). Place the cheese on a shelf so that the air can circulate around it. At first the cheese should be turned every day, then three times a week and later once a week. If any cracks appear cover them with melted lard.

CAERPHILLY-TYPE CHEESE

Ripening Heat 10 litres (2.2 gallons) milk to 32°C (90°F) for cow's milk, 29°C (85°F) for goat's milk. Add 170ml (6fl oz) of cheese starter, and then cover and leave to ripen for 30 minutes.

Renneting Add 1 teaspoon of rennet (diluted with water) to each 10 litres (2.2 gallons) of milk. Stir thoroughly for ½ minute and then topstir (see page 72) until coagulation begins. Cover and leave for 45 minutes, or until the curd is firm.

Cutting Cut the curd as before (see pages 92–93). Turn it over carefully.

Scalding Heat as quickly as possible to 33.5°C (92°F), or for goat's milk 31°C (87°F). Keep the curd at this temperature and stir for 40 minutes. If acidity is developing fast make adjustments as before – heat to 35°C (95°F) and keep at this temperature for 30 minutes. To test whether the curd is ready yet, press your hand firmly on to it; if it is ready the pattern of your skin will appear on the curd and stay there. If this does not happen after 40 minutes (because for example acidity is developing slowly), simply go on stirring at the same temperature until it does.

Draining the whey Let the curd settle in the whey and then pour this off at once. Leave the curd piled to one side of the bucket for 5 minutes and pour off any further whey that has accumulated. Cut the heap of curd into slices vertically and then horizontally (see illustration opposite, left). Spread these slices on one side of the bucket, leaving a channel for the whey to escape. This is made easier if you tip the bucket slightly (see illustration opposite, right). Turn over all the pieces of curd twice in 10 minutes.

Draining the whey.

Salting Break up the curd into walnut-size pieces, and add salt – 30g (1oz) to each 1.8kg (4lb) of curd.

Moulding and pressing Line your mould with a damp cheese cloth, pack it with curd, fold over the muslin, and then place the follower and 1.8kg (4lb) of weights on top. Take the cheese out after 10 minutes and turn it; repeat twice more at 10-minute intervals, then leave the cheese under the weights for 14–16 hours.

Finishing Remove the cheese from the mould and dry off the surface with a dry cloth. Lard and bandage as described on page 97.

Maturing Leave the cheese in a cool place for about 14 days to ripen; remember to turn it daily.

SMALL CHESHIRE CHEESE

Ripening Heat 10 litres (2.2 gallons) milk to 29°C (85°F), and add 115ml (4fl oz) of cheese starter. Leave for 45 minutes.

Renneting Add annatto if required for a red Cheshire colour – ½ teaspoon to 10 litres (2 gallons) of milk. Mix in 1 teaspoon of rennet diluted in water. Stir thoroughly for ½ minute, and then topstir (see page 72) until coagulation takes place. Leave for 45–60 minutes.

Cutting Cut the curd as before (see illustration on page 93); turn it over carefully.

Scalding Raise the temperature of the curd very slowly, taking one hour to reach 34°C (93°F) and stirring all the time. If acidity is developing fast you can heat it more quickly. Then go on stirring until the curd particles are firm and separate easily in your hand.

Draining the whey Let the curd settle for about 15 minutes, then pour off the whey. Leave the curd to mat together for 5 minutes, then cut it into blocks and turn each block over. Do this again twice, then break each block into pieces and turn it again, taking care not to crush the curd. Repeat three times at 10-minute intervals.

Salting Break the curd into walnut-size pieces. Sprinkle salt over it – 30g (1oz) to 1.4kg (3lb) of curd – and mix well. Stir the curd to cool it.

Moulding and pressing Pack the curd into a muslin-lined mould, place a follower and up to 3.6kg (8lb) of weights on top. Remove the cheese after one hour, turn it and put it back in the mould under the weights. The next day turn the cheese again, wrap it in a new cloth and replace it in the mould. Leave for 24 hours.

Finishing Lard and bandage as for the Smallholder cheese (see page 97).

Maturing Leave the cheese to ripen for 4–6 weeks in a cool place. Turn regularly.

COOKING

WITH

HOMEMADE

CHEESE

Cheese is an extremely versatile food and can be used for cooking a variety of dishes. Many of your own favourite cheese recipes can be made with the semi-hard cheeses described in this book. Since you may not be as familiar with recipes using 'soft' cheeses, I have selected a few representative examples to show how it too can be used in cooking. You will be able to collect many more recipes as you progress and experiment.

Use acid-curd cheese or Crowdie for preference; the true soft cheeses such as Coulommiers or Cambridge are best eaten straight, so that their taste, texture, colour and shape can be properly appreciated. Cream cheese can be used in many ways; it is ideal for spreads and dips. Yoghurt too is an important ingredient of many recipes.

CHEESECAKE PIE

(Serves 4)

Shortcrust pastry made with 120g (4oz) flour
120g (4oz) acid-curd cheese
30g (1oz) butter (softened)
60g (2oz) caster sugar
1 egg
30g (1oz) self-raising flour
70ml (⅛ pint) milk
1 teaspoon grated lemon rind

Line a 15cm (6in) flan tin with pastry. Bake 'blind' at 200°C (400°F), gas mark 6, for 15 minutes. (To bake blind line the pastry with aluminium foil – this prevents the pastry rising as it cooks. Remove the foil before filling the pastry case.) Mix together the cheese, soft butter, caster sugar, beaten egg, flour, milk and lemon rind. Spoon the cheese mixture into the flan case and bake for 20–30 minutes at 180°C (350°F), gas mark 4, until the filling has set. Turn off the heat and allow the pie to cool slowly in the oven   this will help to prevent it sinking in the middle. Serve hot or cold.

AUSTRIAN CURD CHEESECAKE

(Serves 4)

60g (2oz) butter
90g (3oz) caster sugar
2 eggs
½ teaspoon vanilla essence
225g (8oz) acid-curd cheese
60g (2oz) self-raising flour
1 tablespoon milk
30g (1oz) sultanas

Grease a 20cm (8in) square shallow tin and dust with flour. You can line it with greaseproof paper to ensure that the cake turns out easily. Cream the butter and sugar. Beat in the eggs, one at a time, and add the vanilla essence. Beat in the cheese until the mixture is light and smooth. Stir in the flour, milk and sultanas and spread evenly in the prepared tin. Bake at 180°C (350°F), gas mark 4, for 40 minutes until the cake is firm and set. Allow the cake to cool in the oven slowly, and then turn out on to a rack. Cut the cake into fingers and dust the top with icing sugar.

CHEESE AND PINEAPPLE DIP

225g (8oz) acid-curd cheese
4 tablespoons single cream
4 tablespoons finely chopped pineapple
Salt and pepper
Chopped red and green peppers

Mix the cheese with the cream and pineapple. Season to taste.
Garnish with red and green peppers. Chill well before serving.

YOGHURT SALAD DRESSING

140g (5oz) natural yoghurt
2 tablespoons single cream
3 teaspoons lemon juice
1 level teaspoon caster sugar
Salt and pepper

Beat together the yoghurt, cream, lemon juice and sugar. Season
to taste with salt and pepper. Chill before using.

CREAM CHEESE AND FRUIT FLAN

(Serves 4)

Shortcrust pastry made with 120g (4oz) flour
120g (4oz) cream cheese
60g (2oz) caster sugar
Fresh soft fruit or tinned fruit
2 tablespoons apricot jam

Line a 15cm (6in) flan tin with pastry. Bake 'blind' at 200°C (400°F),
gas mark 6, until crisp and golden brown. (Line the pastry with
aluminium foil, bake for 15 minutes, then remove the foil and
return the flan to the oven to bake for a further 15 minutes.) Cream
the cheese and sugar together, then spread evenly over the bottom
of the flan case. Chill for at least one hour. Arrange soft or drained
tinned fruit on top of the cheese mixture. Warm the apricot jam with
2 tablespoons of hot water, sieve and then spoon carefully over the
fruit as a glaze.

COEUR A LA CREME

(Serves 4)

225g (8oz) acid-curd cheese
60g (2oz) caster sugar
2 tablespoons double cream
2 egg whites

Sieve the cheese then mix in the sugar and cream. Whisk the egg whites until stiff, then fold into the cheese mixture. Spoon into four individual dishes and chill. Serve with fresh soft fruit and cream.

COEUR A LA CREME LIGHT

(Serves 4)

225g (8oz) acid-curd cheese
140g (5oz) natural yoghurt
Juice of ½ lemon
2 egg whites

Sieve the cheese and mix with the yoghurt and lemon juice. Whisk the egg whites until stiff then fold into the cheese mixture. Spoon into four individual dishes and chill. Serve with fresh soft fruit.

THE
JOYS
of
PERFECT
COOKING

SAVOURY FLAN

(Serves 4)
Shortcrust pastry made with 120g (4oz) flour
120g (4oz) streaky bacon
2 eggs
70ml (1/8 pint) milk
120g (4oz) acid-curd cheese
Salt and pepper

Line a 15cm (6in) flan case with pastry. Cut the bacon rashers into small pieces and fry until cooked. Drain off the fat and arrange the bacon pieces in the bottom of the flan case. Beat together the eggs, milk, cheese, salt and pepper, and pour into the flan case. Bake at 180°C (350°F), gas mark 4, for 30 minutes or until the filling is set and golden brown. Serve hot or cold.

CREAM CHEESE AND YOGHURT DIP

140g (5oz) natural yoghurt
120g (4oz) cream cheese
2 tablespoons finely chopped peeled cucumber
1 level teaspoon paprika
Salt and pepper

Beat the yoghurt into the cheese. Stir in the cucumber and paprika. Season to taste. Chill well before serving.

CHEESE STUFFED TOMATOES

(Serves 4 as a starter)

4 large tomatoes
120g (4oz) acid-curd or cream cheese
1 stick celery, chopped
1 eating apple, chopped
1 spring onion, chopped, or 1 level tablespoon chopped chives
Salt and pepper

Cut the tops off the tomatoes and scoop out the centres. Mix the centres with the other ingredients, and add salt and pepper to taste. When ready to serve divide the mixture between the tomatoes and replace the lids.

SAVOURY CREAM CHEESE FLAN

(Serves 4)

Shortcrust pastry made with 120g (4oz) flour
120g (4oz) cream cheese
Garnishings – sliced cucumber, hard-boiled egg,
onion rings, radishes or ham rolls

Line a 15cm (6in) flan tin with pastry. Bake 'blind' at 200°C (400°F), gas mark 6, until crisp and golden brown. (Line the pastry with aluminium foil, bake for 15 minutes, then remove the foil and return the flan to the oven to bake for a further 15 minutes.) Spread the cream cheese evenly over the bottom of the flan case. Decorate with a selection of the garnishings. Serve very cold with a salad.

CHILLED LEMON CHEESECAKE

(Serves 4)
Biscuit base:
6 digestive biscuits
30g (1oz) butter, softened
30g (1oz) sugar

Filling:
½ pack lemon jelly
1 egg, separated
120g (4oz) acid-curd cheese
140g (5oz) natural yoghurt
lemon rind and the juice from ½ lemon

Break the digestive biscuits into crumbs and mix well with the softened butter and sugar. Line a flan ring with the biscuit-crumb mixture, pressing down well. Put it into the refrigerator to harden. Add 2 tablespoons of hot water to the jelly pieces. Continue to melt the jelly in a bowl over hot water. Allow to cool slightly. Beat in the egg yolk, sieved cheese, yoghurt, lemon rind and juice. Fold in the whisked egg white, and pour the mixture into the biscuit crust. Replace in the refrigerator to set, preferably overnight.

OTHER

DAIRY

PRODUCTS

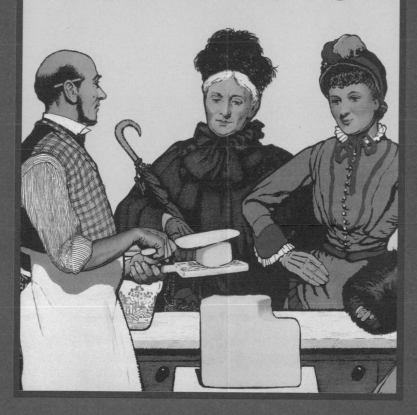

YOGHURT

Yoghurt is a cultured milk. It has only been popular in this country for 50–60 years, but different cultured milks have been consumed for centuries in Eastern Europe and in the countries of the Near, Middle and Far East.

Cultured milk is produced by the action of bacterial micro-organisms that change the lactose (milk sugar) into lactic acid. The result is an acid-curd. In hot countries these soured or cultured milks are considered the best way to consume milk, since the lactic acid acts as a preservative and keeps the milk in a palatable form.

There is a great range of cultured milks; yoghurt, for example, is the traditional cultured milk of the Balkans – Greece, Turkey and Bulgaria. The differences in taste and texture between the various forms of cultured milk depend partly on the type of milk used – it may come from cows, goats, sheep, buffaloes or even mares – and partly on the type of bacterial micro-organism present; each type provides its own characteristic flavour. The flavour and texture of yoghurt is imparted by a culture which consists of equal proportions of *Lactobacillus bulgaricus* and *Streptococcus thermophilus*.

Live yoghurt

Some people believe that only yoghurts labelled 'live' or 'true' contain the live yoghurt culture; this is not so. All yoghurts sold in the UK are made from a live culture. After incubation the yoghurt is cooled and then kept at a low temperature. This arrests the growth of the culture but does not kill it.

Other Dairy Products

Food value

Various therapeutic benefits have been attributed to yoghurt, but the original theory that yoghurt possesses unique properties that ensure a long and healthy life has not been proved. Nevertheless, because it is made from milk, yoghurt is an excellent food. Most commercially produced yoghurts are made from a skimmed-milk base with added dried skimmed milk powder producing a thick yoghurt and a low fat content. The fruit yoghurts have added fruit and sugar of course, so the milk nutrients are reduced accordingly.

Yoghurt is a food that appeals to and can be eaten by people of all ages. Because it is easily digested it is very suitable for babies (from about 6 months onwards) and for old people.

Making yoghurt at home

There are various yoghurt-making machines on the market and you may wish to invest in one. However these are relatively expensive and other suitable incubators can be improvised.

You will need a saucepan, a tablespoon, a thermometer and a room thermometer, a suitable container for incubating the yoghurt, a fresh carton of yoghurt or yoghurt culture and, of course, the milk.

First sterilize all the equipment as described on page 38. Raw or pasteurized milk should be boiled for one minute first to denature the whey proteins – this is key to producing a stable thick yoghurt that does not separate into curds and whey when stirred after setting. Cool the milk to 43°C (110°F); it should be stirred carefully to prevent a skin forming while cooling. Alternatively, sterilized or ultra-heat-treated milk can be used for yoghurt (although not for making cheese); these types of milk need not be boiled, but can just be heated to 43°C (110°F).

Now add 15ml (1 tablespoon) of natural yoghurt to each pint of milk and mix well. Make sure from the date code that the yoghurt you use is as fresh as possible. Yoghurt caps should be secure and not 'blown'. Buy from chilled cabinets only. Alternatively, a yoghurt culture can be used – this is widely available online and comes in many different forms depending on your preference.

Pour the milk into a suitable container or containers – you can use old yoghurt cartons (washed and sterilized) for individual yoghurts. Cover and leave in a warm place for 3–4 hours to allow the yoghurt to set. The yoghurt culture is thermophilic (likes higher temperatures). It needs a temperature of about 43°C (110°F) at which to grow; cheese starter generally prefers moderate temperatures to thrive, i.e 20–38°C (mesophilic cultures). Your linen cupboard may maintain a temperature as high as this – check with a room thermometer – or use a wooden box incubator as described in the section on starter cultivation (see pages 54–55).

Alternatively, a wide-necked vacuum flask can be used as an incubator; it will maintain the temperature of the milk. Pour the milk into the flask and leave this in a warm place for 3–4 hours to allow the yoghurt to set. Remember that it will need careful cleaning and sterilization afterwards. Or you can use a baby's bottle warmer. Find the appropriate setting as described before in the section on starter cultivation page 54 – I find, with my bottle warmer, that a temperature of 43°C (110°F) is reached at setting no. 1. The bottle warmer, however, will only hold a baby's bottle or similar sized container, so you will not be able to make more than a small quantity – 300ml (½ pint) – at a time. Again, the yoghurt will take about three hours to set.

When the yoghurt has set, it should be placed in the refrigerator or a cool place until eaten. The yoghurt incubated in a vacuum flask should at this stage be poured into another container. You can make your own fruit yoghurt by stirring in fruit or jam after it has set, or sweeten it to taste by adding sugar or honey.

If you use a bought yoghurt as the initial culture it is wise to buy a new one each time you make yoghurt. Contamination could occur if a portion of the homemade yoghurt is saved to act as a 'starter' for the next batch. Making yoghurt at home is still inexpensive, since a small carton of yoghurt can be used to make a large amount of fresh yoghurt. If you use a yoghurt culture, this can be recultivated and maintained in the same way as described for cheese starter (pages 49–53), but remember to incubate it at 43°C (110°F).

CREAM

Cream contains most of the milk fat together with a proportion of the other milk constituents. It is produced from whole milk by separation; the fat which consists of many tiny fat globules is lighter than the rest of the milk, and so the cream rises naturally to the surface. The amount of cream in the milk, and its colour, depend largely on the breed of cow; milk from the Channel Island breeds and South Devon cows has a high fat content and the cream is a rich yellow colour.

Commercial dairies separate cream by centrifugal force in a mechanical separator. Creams of varying butterfat content can be produced by this process and those available on the market include:

Half cream (fat content of 10–12 per cent). This may be called 'top of the milk' and is a pouring cream. Most shop-bought milk is homogenized these days, which emulsifies the fat or cream into the milk, so it is rare to get top of the milk.

Single cream (18 per cent) A pouring cream ideal for coffee, soup and desserts. It will not whip as the fat content is too low.

Long-life cream (UHT) This has undergone ultra heat treatment (UHT) so that it lasts longer. It is available in cartons which do not need to be kept in the fridge but should be consumed quickly once opened.

Whipping cream (35 per cent) The best cream for whipping; it should whip up to twice its volume.

Double cream (48 per cent) A rich pouring cream; it will whip but better results are obtained if a tablespoon of milk is added to each pint of cream. There is also a 'thick' double cream which is heavily homogenized and will not whip.

Clotted cream (55 per cent) A thick cream with its own special 'nutty' flavour and golden yellow colour. It is made by a process of scalding the cream (described page 128) and is produced chiefly in the West Country.

Producing cream at home

If you have a ready supply of raw milk you may like to separate your own cream. You will need a large shallow pan and a hand skimmer (see illustration below). See pages 138–140) for suppliers. If you cannot obtain the skimmer, a thin-edged saucer can be used. Pour the warm milk, fresh from the cow, into the pan and leave it to stand for 24 hours in a cool place, so that the fat comes to the surface and forms a thin layer of cream. If you are using goat's milk you will have to leave it for longer since the fat globules are smaller than those in cow's milk, and the cream consequently takes longer to rise. Do not leave any strong-smelling substance near the milk as cream readily absorbs flavours.

Cream pan and skimmer

Now skim the cream using a sharp-edged perforated skimmer, which allows the skimmed milk to drain back into the pan. Start by breaking it off at the pan edges – it will peel back like a thick skin. There will be a great deal of variation in the consistency of the cream produced by this method, and some of the fat will be left in the skimmed milk. However, you will gradually become more expert. The cream you obtain this way should have a butterfat content of about 50 per cent – similar to double cream. If you require a thinner cream, for example to make single-cream cheese, you can dilute the cream with an equal quantity of skimmed milk.

Pasteurization of home-produced cream

It is advisable to pasteurize home-produced cream to make sure it is safe and free from contaminating organisms. Pour the cream into a bucket and place this in a larger container filled with boiling water. Raise the temperature of the cream to 63°C (145°F), and hold it at this temperature for 30 minutes. Stir frequently to ensure even heating. Then cool at once to 4.5°C (40°F) by putting the bucket of cream into cold running water.

How to whip cream

It is important that the cream is aged and cooled before it is whipped. During the pasteurization the fat melts, and so aging for at least 24 hours at 4.5°C (40°F) is essential to allow most of the fat to resolidify. This also applies to bought cream; it is advisable to age this first before whipping it because it may have become warm on the journey home from the shops or on the doorstep. After aging you will notice that the cream is thicker.

The cream, whisk and bowl should be really cold. The equipment can be cooled in cold water, or left in the refrigerator for a time before whipping. A hand balloon whisk will give the best results.

Whip the cream quickly at first until it takes on a matt finish, and then slowly until it stands in peaks. Great care should be taken not to overwhip as this will turn the cream into butter!

Making clotted cream

The simplest method is to scald the cream in a double saucepan (or a bowl in a saucepan of boiling water). Heat the cream to 77–88°C (170–190°F) and keep it at this temperature until the top of the cream becomes thick and crusty, with a wrinkled appearance. This may take from ½–1 hour depending on the quantity of cream. The cream should be stirred occasionally at first to ensure even heating. Since the cream is being scalded it does not require prior pasteurization.

When it is ready, remove the top saucepan or bowl and cool it rapidly by placing it in cold water. Leave it in the refrigerator or a cool place for 24 hours to 'age' it. The clotted cream can then be packed in small glass jars or plastic containers, and should be kept in the refrigerator until eaten within 4–5 days.

If you wish to make your own clotted cream from bought cream, use double cream.

BUTTER

Whereas milk is an emulsion of fat globules in a watery solution, butter is an emulsion of water in solidified fat. It is obtained from cream by churning; the churning action causes the fat globules to merge and form butter granules.

Making butter at home

You can easily make butter at home with an ordinary hand or electric beater, but there are small hand or electric butter churns available if you wish to invest in one. You will also need a wooden board, and scotch hands (see illustration below) to work the butter.

First separate your cream and keep it cool until ready for use. You can use either fresh cream, or ripened cream which is slightly sour. Ripened cream does give better results. If you are making cheese you will have cheese starter available and can use this to ripen the cream; alternatively you can obtain special butter starter. Add about 140ml (5fl oz) of starter to each gallon of cream and leave it in a warm place or incubator about 21°C (70°F) – for a good 12 hours (see the section on starter cultivation pages 53–55). After ripening, cool the cream to 4.5–7°C (40–45°F) for several hours to allow the fat to harden again before churning.

Scotch hands

The churning temperature is most important – it should be between 10°C and 18°C (50°F and 65°F) depending on the season of the year: lower in hot summer weather and higher in cooler weather. Bring your cream to the correct temperature. The mixing bowl or churn jar can be stood in a larger bowl of cold or warm water as necessary to obtain the correct temperature. The wooden board and scotch hands should be stood in cold water until used.

Pour the cream into the bowl or churn (see illustration below), filling it not more than half full. You can add a few drops of annatto colouring if you wish. Now whisk or churn the cream until it thickens and begins to separate into butter grains and buttermilk; if you use an electric beater, set it at a slow speed. At this stage add some cold water – about 10°C (50°F) – and churn again. This

Small hand butter churn

is known as the 'breaking' water and helps to separate and round off the butter grains. If necessary add some more cold water to help the cream to 'break', but the total breaking water used should not amount to more than a quarter of the quantity of cream. Churn until the granules reach the size of wheat grains.

Pour off the buttermilk and save this. Pour cold water over the butter grains to wash them; again the water should be colder than the churning temperature. Whisk or churn for a few seconds, and then run off the water. Repeat the washings until the water runs off as a clear liquid; it is important that all the buttermilk is washed out of the butter, otherwise the butter will not keep and may go rancid.

Collect the butter from the bowl or jar by straining it through a muslin cloth. Press out the water, and if the butter is soft leave it in a cool place to harden a little.

The butter must now be well worked to remove as much water as possible, so that it will keep. Place the butter on a wooden board and pat it with the scotch hands or other suitable utensils to press out the water. Pat it down into a thin layer, fold it over and pat down again. If you slope the board slightly the water can run off. Try to keep the butter as cool as possible. Salt can be worked into the butter at the same time, at the rate of 1–2 teaspoons to every 450g (1lb) of butter, according to taste. Finally pat the butter into shape and wrap it in greaseproof paper. Keep it in the freezer until you want to use it as this greatly improves shelf life and avoids butter becoming rancid.

The utensils used in buttermaking should be rinsed, washed and sterilized as before; wooden equipment, however, should be washed in washing-soda crystals only since detergent makes the wood sticky and could taint the butter.

If you wish to make your own butter from bought cream you can use whipping or double cream, but it will be fairly expensive butter!

Buttermilk

The buttermilk contains most of the other milk constituents in a diluted form, and so has some food value; it would be a waste to throw it away. It is a very refreshing drink when cold, and can be used in baking. It is, for example, used to make soda bread, and can also be used to make scones. If you have used ripened cream for buttermaking, the buttermilk will contain some of the culture. You can make your own cultured buttermilk by leaving this in a warm place or incubator at 21°C (70°F) to coagulate and thicken.

The cultured buttermilk that is available commercially used to be made from buttermilk, but now most of it is made from skimmed milk. A bacterial culture is added and the milk incubated until the desired acidity is reached.

POSTSCRIPT

By now you will be familiar with many of the cheesemaking processes and will perhaps already have discovered that it is a relatively easy craft once you have collected together your equipment, mastered a few techniques such as sterilization and the recultivation of starter, and experimented a few times.

Indeed experimentation and improvisation may be the key to your own cheesemaking. The recipes and methods given in this book have worked well for me, but there is no reason why, having mastered the basic principles, you should not experiment to find your own recipes both for soft and hard cheeses. Indeed you will soon find that no two cheeses turn out exactly the same even if you do follow the same recipe each time. Half the fun of cheesemaking is not knowing exactly how successful you have been until you sit down to taste your finished cheese.

The equipment suggested is simple and works well for small amounts of milk, but you may be able to improvise bigger and better equipment if you are dealing with larger milk quantities.

Whatever sort of cheese you are making, its nutritional value will be high. So in making cheese you are not only enjoying a fascinating craft, but are producing an essential and extremely satisfying commodity for yourself and your family.

Susan Ogilvy

GLOSSARY

You may be unfamiliar with some of the terms used in the book. Here they are listed alphabetically with a simple explanation of their meaning in the context of this book, and a page reference to where further details can be found in the text.

Acid curd Formed by the action of a relatively high acidity on the milk protein; the protein separates and a curd is formed in which the liquid whey is held (compare with rennet curd) (see pages 13 and 14)

Acidity The amount of acid in the milk; the milk's sourness. Acidity is very important in the cheesemaking process and is produced by the lactic-acid bacteria present in the milk (see pages 13–15).

Aging cream Keeping cream at a cold temperature – 4.5°C (40°F) – for at least 24 hours. During pasteurization the fat in the cream melts and aging is necessary to resolidify it, and so ensure good results when whipping it (see page 125).

Annatto A natural vegetable extract used to give a reddish or orange colour to cheese or butter (see page 48).

Antibiotic A substance capable of destroying micro-organisms (see page 58).

Bacteria Microscopic unicellular organisms found almost everywhere; some types are beneficial – for example the cheesemaking bacteria – and some are harmful and cause disease (see pages 14, 20 and 26).

Calcium A mineral element, greyish white in colour; a major constituent of bones and teeth. Milk and cheese are rich sources of calcium in our diet and owe their white colour to its presence (see page 14).

Casein A milk protein which has the ability to precipitate when rennet is added or the milk becomes very acid (see page 13).

Cheese starter A special bacterial culture used to produce acid during cheesemaking and to contribute to the flavour of the cheese. The bacteria use the milk sugar, lactose, for growth and change it to lactic acid (see page 49).

Emulsion A watery liquid with oily or fatty particles suspended in it (see page 129).

Enzymes Naturally occurring chemical compounds which help bring about chemical changes (see page 20).

Freeze-dried culture A culture which has been frozen and then placed in a vacuum chamber and the air pumped out so that the ice formed on freezing evaporates directly as vapour without turning back into moisture. The culture is reactivated when added to liquid milk (see page 58).

Homogenization A process in which the fat globules in milk and cream are broken down to smaller particles and evenly distributed so that the fat does not rise to the surface.

Incubation The provision of a constant warm temperature to allow the bacterial culture to grow (see pages 53–56).

Junket A semi-solid curd pudding, rather like custard, formed when rennet is added to warm milk (see page 13).

Lactose The milk sugar; it can be changed to lactic acid by certain bacteria, thereby increasing the acidity of the milk (see page 14).

Moulds Minute fungi which exhibit a woolly or furry growth (see page 23–24).

Pasteurization A mild heat treatment – the milk is heated to 71°C (160°F) for 15 seconds and then cooled rapidly. This kills all disease organisms and most lactic acid-producing bacteria (see pages 14, 24 and 42–44).

Proteins Organic compounds which form an important part of all living organisms; they are essential constituents of the diet of animals (see pages 13–14).

Rennet A substance containing rennin and other enzymes which is found in the stomach of young mammals and has the property of clotting milk (see page 46).

Rennet curd The curd formed when rennet is added to milk (compare with acid curd) (see page 14).

Starter culture Milk mixed with specific bacteria which create the acidity needed for cheesemaking (see pages 18 and 49).

Sterilized milk Milk which has been homogenized, then heat-treated to above boiling point – not less than 100°C (212°F) for 20–30 minutes. This process destroys bacteria and other micro-organisms more completely than pasteurization. The heat treatment gives the milk a creamy colour and a slight caramel flavour (see page 14).

Sterilization The destruction of all micro-organisms by heat or chemical means (see page 38–39).

Topstir Stir the top 6mm (¼in) of milk very firmly and smoothly after the addition of rennet until coagulation takes place. This prevents the fat from rising to the surface (see page 72).

Ultra-heat-treated milk (UHT) Milk which is heated to very high temperature for a very short time – 132°C (270°F) for one second. This heat treatment sterilizes the milk but does not affect its taste and colour. Aseptically packed in aluminium foil packs, it keeps for several months if unopened. Known as 'long-life milk' (see pages 14, 42 and 119).

Whey The liquid produced when milk clots. It is held in the curd and released gradually when the curd is cut, heated, drained or pressed. Consists mostly of water and lactose together with a small proportion of other milk constituents (see pages 14–15, 18–19, 63–64 and 85).

Yoghurt A cultured milk product produced by the growth of 'yoghurt' lactic-acid bacteria; an acid curd is formed (see pages 118–121).

SUPPLIERS

UK

Ascott Dairy
Moulds, cultures, equipment.
Carriage House
Forde Close
Newton Abbot
Devon TQ12 4E7
Tel: 01626 880894
www.ascott-dairy.co.uk

Alpma GB LTD
Cheese moulds.
1 Devinshire Business Park
Knights Park Road
Basingstoke
Hampshire RG21 6XN
Tel: 01256 467177
www.alpma.co.uk

Goat Nutrition Ltd
Goat supplies, milking
equipment, secondhand cheese
and dairy equipment, cultures,
wax and packaging.
Unit B/C Smarden Buisness Estate
Monks Hill
Smarden
Kent TN27 8QL
Tel: 01233 770780
www.gnltd.co.uk

Jaap De Jonge (Jongia (Uk) Ltd
Equipment, hobbiest online shop,
educational visits to European
cheesemakers.
Jongia (UK) Ltd.
23 Prospect Lane
Solihull B91 1HN
Tel:01217444844
www.jongiauk.com

Moorlands Cheesemakers Ltd
Equipment and cultures.
Lorien House
South Street
Castle Cary
Somerset BA7 7ES
Tel: 01963 350634
www.cheesemaking.co.uk

Nisbets
Catering Equipment (next day
delivery) digital thermometers
and lots more.
Fourth Way
Avonmouth
Bristol BS11 8TB
Tel: 0845 1405555
www.nisbets.co.uk

Orchard Valley Dairy Supplies
Cultures, rennet, acidity test
chemicals, wax and technical
help.
4 Lower Teme Buisness Park
Burford
Tenbury Wells
Worcs WR15 8SZ
Tel: 01584 811137
www.orchard-dairy.co.uk

*Specialist Cheesemakers
Association*
For artisan cheesemakers, help
with technical and practical
problems.
17 Clerkenwell Green
London EC1R ODP
Tel: 020 72253 2114
www.specialistcheesemakers.
co.uk

Red Devon Cheese Company
Small cheese presses, short
courses.
Hagley Bridge Farm
Waterrow
Somerset TA4 2BQ
Tel: 01984 629026
www.reddevoncheesecompany.
co.uk

British Goat Society
Contact the secretary on
01434240866 or
secretary@allgoats.com
www.allgoats.com

US

The Beverage People
Cheese-making kits, cultures,
rennet, moulds, presses, tools and
more.
1845 Piner Road
Santa Rosa CA95403
Tel: 800 544 1863

The Cheese Connection
Cultures, moulds, presses, wax,
tools and recipes.
Seattle, Washington
Tel: 844 287 3711
www.stores.cheeseconnection.net

The Cheesemaker
Cheese-making kits, presses and
ingredients as well as butter- and
yoghurt-making supplies.
11611 North Grace Court
Mequon WI 53092
Tel: 414 745 5483
www.thecheesemaker.com

Cultures for Health
Cheese starters, rennet and
cheese-making kits.
1801 N Louise Drive
Sioux Falls SD 57107
Tel: 800 962 1959
www.culturesforhealth.com

Hoegger Supply Company
Cheese-making moulds, presses,
kits, cultures, skimmers,
thermometers, cheese cloths
and more as well as butter- and
yoghurt-making supplies.
Tel: 800 221 4628
www.hoeggerfarmyard.com

Lehmans
Mesophilic cheese starter.
PO Box 270
Kidron OH 44636
Tel: 888 438 5346
www.lehmans.com

Midwest Supplies
Cheese-making kits and starter
cultures.
5825 Excelsior Blvd
Minneapolis MN 55416
Tel: 888 449 2739
www.medwestsupplies.com

*New England Cheesemaking
Supply Company*
Cheese-making kits, workshops
and ingredients including
mesophilic starter and rennet.
54B Whately Road
South Deerfield MA 01373
Tel: 413 397 2012
www.cheesemaking.com

Canada

Glengarry Cheesemaking
Cultures for cheese and yoghurt
making, moulds, rennet, cultures,
wax and more.
PO Box 190
5926 HWY 34
Lancaster ON, K0C 1N0
Tel: 888 816 0903
www.glengarrycheesemaking.
on.ca

Make Cheese
Cheese-making kits, cultures,
rennet, wax, equipment and
classes.
Kettle Crossing Farm
Bergen AB, near Calgary
Tel: 403 689 3552
www.makecheese.ca

INDEX

PICTURE CREDITS & ACKNOWLEDGMENTS

The Author would like to thank the following people for the valuable help and advice they provided in the writing of this book:

R. Osborne of the Milk. Marketing Board; J. W. Hughes and Miss D. F. Williams of ADAS, Ministry of Agriculture, Fisheries and Food; B. A. Galloway of the Somerset College of Agriculture and Horticulture; Miss M. Johnston of Lackham College of Agriculture, Wiltshire; A L. Walker of the West of Scotland Agricultural College; Mrs L. Hetherington of the British Goat Society; and the many readers of *Farmers Weekly* who wrote to tell her of their own experiences in cheesemaking.

The following books and leaflets were particularly useful: *Home Made Cheeses*, A 'Farm Woman's Library' Book, Hulton Press, 1957; *The Backyard Dairy Book*, published by Whole Earth Tools, 1972; *The Story of Cheesemaking in Britain*, by V. Cheke, Routledge and Kegan Paul, 1959; *Dictionary of Dairying*, by J. G. Davis, Leonard Hill, 1965; *Dairy Work for Goatkeepers*, published by the British Goat Society, 1973; *A Handbook of Dairy Foods*, issued by the National Dairy Council; *Cooking with Yoghurt, Cultured Cream and Soft Cheese*, by Bee Nilson, Pelham Books, 1973; and the advisory leaflets issued by the Ministry of Agriculture, Fisheries and Food: Soft Cheese, Cream Cheese, Cream, Clotted Cream and Starters for Cheesemaking.

The Author and Publishers would also like to thank John Walters for the line drawings. Other images are credited as follows:
Page 2, 21, 27, 29, 43, 59, 103, 110 © Mary Evans Picture Library. Page 11 © Mary Evans / The National Archives, London, England. Page 41, 126–127 © Mary Evans Picture Library / Onslow Auctions Limited. Page 66 © Mary Evans / Retrograph Collection. Page 87, 122 © Mary Evans Picture Library / John Maclellan.
Page 16 © Fry Art Gallery, Saffron Walden, Essex, UK / Bridgeman Images. Page 61 © Bridgeman Images. Page 82 © Look and Learn / Bridgeman Images. Page 96 and 117 © Manchester Art Gallery, UK / Bridgeman Images.
Page 8, 78, 91 © Transport for London.